Laboratory Man

Prentice Hall

Biology

Prentice
Hall

Upper Saddle River, New Jersey
Glenview, Illinois
Needham, Massachusetts

Laboratory Manual B

Prentice Hall
Biology

ISBN 0-13-044171-6

8 9 10   05 04

Contents

Unit 3   Cells

Unit 4   Genetics

Unit 5   Evolution

Unit 6   Microorganisms and Fungi

Unit 7   Plants

Unit 8   Invertebrates

Unit 9   Chordates

Unit 10   The Human Body

Safety in the Biology Laboratory

Working in the biology laboratory can be interesting, exciting, and rewarding. But it can also be quite dangerous if you are not serious and alert and if proper safety precautions are not taken at all times. You are responsible for maintaining an enjoyable, instructional, and safe environment in the biology laboratory. Unsafe practices endanger not only you but the people around you as well.

Read the following information about safety in the biology laboratory carefully. Review applicable safety information before you begin each Laboratory Investigation. If you have any questions about safety or laboratory procedures, be sure to ask your teacher.

Safety Symbol Guide

All the investigations in this laboratory manual have been designed with safety in mind. If you follow the instructions, you should have a safe and interesting year in the laboratory. Before beginning any investigation, make sure you read the safety rules on pages 8–11 of *Laboratory Manual B*.

The safety symbols shown on page 8 are used throughout *Laboratory Manual B*. They appear first next to the Safety section of an investigation and then next to certain steps in an investigation where specific safety precautions are required. The symbols alert you to the need for special safety precautions. The description of each symbol indicates the precaution(s) you should take whenever you see the symbol in an investigation.

Safety Symbols

These symbols alert you to possible dangers.

Safety Goggles Always wear safety goggles to protect your eyes in any activity involving chemicals, flames, or heating, or the possibility of broken glassware.

Laboratory Apron Wear a laboratory apron to protect your skin and clothing.

Breakage You are working with breakable materials, such as glassware. Handle breakable materials with care. Do not touch broken glassware.

Heat-resistant Gloves Use hand protection when handling hot materials. Hot equipment or hot water can cause burns. Do not touch hot objects with your bare hands.

Plastic Gloves Wear disposable plastic gloves to protect yourself from chemicals or organisms that could be harmful. Keep your hands away from your face. Dispose of the gloves according to your teacher's instructions at the end of the activity.

Heating Use a clamp or tongs to pick up hot glassware. Do not touch hot objects with your bare hands.

Sharp Object Pointed-tip scissors, scalpels, knives, needles, pins, or tacks can cut or puncture your skin. Always direct a sharp edge or point away from yourself and others. Use sharp instruments only as directed.

Electric Shock Avoid the possibility of electric shock. Never use electrical equipment around water, or when equipment is wet or your hands are wet. Be sure cords are untangled and cannot trip anyone. Disconnect the equipment when it is not in use.

Corrosive Chemical Avoid getting acids or other corrosive chemicals on your skin or clothing, or in your eyes. Do not inhale the vapors. Wash your hands when you are finished with the activity.

Poison Do not let any poisonous chemical come in contact with your skin, and do not inhale its vapors. Wash your hands when you are finished with the activity.

Physical Safety When an experiment involves physical activity, take precautions to avoid injuring yourself or others. Follow instructions from your teacher. Alert your teacher if there is any reason you should not participate in the activity.

Animal Safety Treat live animals with care to avoid harming the animals or yourself. Working with animal parts or preserved animals also may require caution. Wash your hands when you are finished.

Plant Safety Handle plants only as directed by your teacher. If you are allergic to certain plants, tell your teacher before doing an activity in which plants are used. Avoid touching poisonous plants or plants with thorns. Wash your hands when you are finished with the activity.

Flames You may be working with flames from a Bunsen burner, candle, or matches. Tie back loose hair and clothing. Follow instructions from your teacher about lighting and extinguishing flames.

No Flames Flammable materials may be present. Make sure no flames, sparks, or exposed heat sources are present.

Fumes When poisonous or unpleasant vapors may be involved, work in a ventilated area. Avoid inhaling vapors directly. Only test an odor when directed to do so by your teacher, and use a wafting motion to direct the vapor toward your nose.

Disposal Chemicals and other used materials must be disposed of safely. Follow the instructions from your teacher.

Hand Washing Wash your hands thoroughly. Use antibacterial soap and warm water. Lather both sides of your hands and between your fingers. Rinse well.

General Safety Awareness You may see this symbol when none of the other symbols appears. In this case, follow the specific instructions provided. You may also see this symbol when you are asked to develop your own procedure. Have your teacher approve your plan before you go further.

Science Safety Rules

One of the first things a scientist learns is that working in the laboratory can be an exciting experience. But the laboratory can also be quite dangerous if proper safety rules are not followed at all times. To prepare yourself for a safe year in the laboratory, read over the following safety rules. Then read them a second time. Make sure you understand each rule. If you do not, ask your teacher to explain any rules you are unsure of.

Dress Code

1. Many materials in the laboratory can cause eye injury. To protect yourself from possible injury, wear safety goggles whenever you are working with chemicals, burners, or any substance that might get into your eyes. Never wear contact lenses in the laboratory.

2. Wear a laboratory apron or coat whenever you are working with chemicals or heated substances.

3. Tie back long hair to keep your hair away from any chemicals, burners and candles, or other laboratory equipment.

4. Remove or tie back any article of clothing or jewelry that can hang down and touch chemicals and flames. Do not wear sandals or open-toed shoes in the laboratory. Never walk around the laboratory barefoot or in stocking feet.

General Safety Rules

5. Be serious and alert when working in the laboratory. Never "horse around" in the laboratory.

6. Be prepared to work when you arrive in the laboratory. Be sure that you understand the procedure to be employed in any laboratory investigation and the possible hazards associated with it.

7. Read all directions for an investigation several times. Follow the directions exactly as they are written. If you are in doubt about any part of the investigation, ask your teacher for assistance.

8. Never perform activities that are not authorized by your teacher. Obtain permission before "experimenting" on your own.

9. Never handle any equipment unless you have specific permission.

10. Take extreme care not to spill any material in the laboratory. If spills occur, ask your teacher immediately about the proper cleanup procedure. Never simply pour chemicals or other substances into the sink or trash container.

11. Never eat or taste anything or apply cosmetics in the laboratory unless directed to do so. This includes food, drinks, candy, and gum, as well as chemicals. Wash your hands before and after performing every investigation.

12. Know the location and proper use of safety equipment such as the fire extinguisher, fire blanket, first-aid kit, safety shower, and eyewash station.

13. Notify your teacher of any medical problems you may have, such as allergies or asthma.

14. Keep your laboratory area clean and free of unnecessary books, papers, and equipment.

First Aid

15. Report all accidents, no matter how minor, to your teacher immediately.

16. Learn what to do in case of specific accidents such as getting acid in your eyes or on your skin. (Rinse acids off your body with lots of water.)

17. Become aware of the location of the first-aid kit. Your teacher should administer any required first aid due to injury. Or your teacher may send you to the school nurse or call a physician.

18. Know where and how to report an accident or fire. Find out the location of the fire extinguisher, phone, and fire alarm. Keep a list of important phone numbers such as the fire department and school

nurse near the phone. Report any fires to your teacher at once.

Heating and Fire Safety

19. Never use a heat source such as a candle or burner without wearing safety goggles.

20. Never heat a chemical you are not instructed to heat. A chemical that is harmless when cool can be dangerous when heated.

21. Maintain a clean work area and keep all materials away from flames.

22. Never reach across a flame.

23. Make sure you know how to light a Bunsen burner. (Your teacher will demonstrate the proper procedure for lighting a burner.) If the flame leaps out of a burner toward you, turn the gas off immediately. Do not touch the burner. It may be hot. And never leave a lighted burner unattended.

24. Point a test tube or bottle that is being heated away from you and others. Chemicals can splash or boil out of a heated test tube.

25. Never heat a liquid in a closed container. The expanding gases produced may blow the container apart, injuring you or others.

26. Never pick up a container that has been heated without first holding the back of your hand near it. If you can feel the heat on the back of your hand, the container may be too hot to handle. Use a clamp, tongs, or heat-resistant gloves when handling hot containers.

Using Chemicals Safely

27. Never mix chemicals for the "fun of it." You might produce a dangerous, possibly explosive, substance.

28. Never touch, taste, or smell a chemical that you do not know for a fact is harmless. Many chemicals are poisonous. If you are instructed to note the fumes in an investigation, gently wave your hand over the opening of a container and direct the fumes toward your nose. Do not inhale the fumes directly from the container.

29. Use only those chemicals needed in the investigation. Keep all lids closed when a chemical is not being used. Notify your teacher whenever chemicals are spilled.

30. Dispose of all chemicals as instructed by your teacher. To avoid contamination, never return chemicals to their original containers.

31. Be extra careful when working with acids or bases. Pour such chemicals over the sink, not over your workbench.

32. When diluting an acid, pour the acid into water. Never pour water into the acid.

33. Rinse any acids off your skin or clothing with water. Immediately notify your teacher of any acid spill.

Using Glassware Safely

34. Never force glass tubing into a rubber stopper. A turning motion and lubricant will be helpful when inserting glass tubing into rubber stoppers or rubber tubing. Your teacher will demonstrate the proper way to insert glass tubing.

35. Never heat glassware that is not thoroughly dry. Use a wire screen to protect glassware from any flame.

36. Keep in mind that hot glassware will not appear hot. Never pick up glassware without first checking to see if it is hot.

37. If you are instructed to cut glass tubing, fire polish the ends immediately to remove sharp edges.

38. Never use broken or chipped glassware. If glassware breaks, notify your teacher and dispose of the glassware in the proper trash container.

39. Never eat or drink from laboratory glassware. Clean glassware thoroughly before putting it away.

Using Sharp Instruments

40. Handle scalpels or razor blades with extreme care. Never cut material toward you; cut away from you.

41. Be careful when handling sharp, pointed objects such as scissors, pins, and dissecting probes.

42. Notify your teacher immediately if you cut yourself or receive a cut.

Handling Living Organisms

43. No investigations that will cause pain, discomfort, or harm to mammals, birds, reptiles, fish, and amphibians should be done in the classroom or at home.

44. Treat all living things with care and respect. Do not touch any organism in the classroom or laboratory unless given permission to do so. Many plants are poisonous or have thorns, and even tame animals may bite or scratch if alarmed.

45. Animals should be handled only if necessary. If an animal is excited or frightened, pregnant, feeding, or with its young, special handling is required.

46. Your teacher will instruct you as to how to handle each species that may be brought into the classroom.

47. Treat all microorganisms as if they were harmful. Use antiseptic procedure, as directed by your teacher, when working with microbes. Dispose of microbes as your teacher directs.

48. Clean your hands thoroughly after handling animals or the cage containing animals.

49. Wear gloves when handling small mammals. Report animal bites or stings to your teacher at once.

End-of-Investigation Rules

50. When an investigation is completed, clean up your work area and return all equipment to its proper place.

51. Wash your hands after every investigation.

52. Turn off all burners before leaving the laboratory. Check that the gas line leading to the burner is off as well.

Safety Contract

Once you have read all the safety information on pages 7–11 in *Laboratory Manual B* and are sure you understand all the rules, fill out the safety contract that follows. Signing this contract tells your teacher that you are aware of the rules of the laboratory. Return your signed contract to your teacher. You will not be allowed to work in the laboratory until you have returned your signed contract.

SAFETY CONTRACT

I, _____, have read the

Safety in the Biology Laboratory section on pages 7–11 in *Biology*

Laboratory Manual B. I understand its contents completely, and agree to

follow all the safety rules and guidelines that have been established in

each of the following areas:

(please check)

☐ Dress Code   ☐ Using Glassware Safely
☐ General Safety Rules   ☐ Using Sharp Instruments
☐ First Aid   ☐ Handling Living Organisms
☐ Heating and Fire Safety   ☐ End-of-Investigation Rules
☐ Using Chemicals Safely

Signature _____ Date _____

How to Use the Laboratory Manual

This is probably the most exciting time in history to be studying biology. The science of biology is progressing rapidly. Biology is directly related to many of today's most important news stories. Cloning of animals; AIDS; animal rights; genetic fingerprinting; acid rain; and efforts to save endangered species all involve biology.

In order to gain a working knowledge of biology, you need to understand some of the processes that scientists use to find answers to problems. The Laboratory Investigations and activities in *Laboratory Manual B* enable you to learn about and practice methods used by scientists in their quest to increase human knowledge.

In each Laboratory Investigation, your objective is to solve a problem using scientific methods. Each Laboratory Investigation follows a standard outline that will help you tackle the problem in a systematic and organized manner.

Introduction The Introduction provides information you will need to complete the investigation, and ties the Laboratory Investigation to concepts discussed in the textbook. The Introduction corresponds to the first step in any scientific work—gathering information about the topic so that you can develop a hypothesis.

Problem This section presents a problem in the form of a question. Your job is to solve the problem based on your observations.

Pre-Lab Discussion After reading the Laboratory Investigation, answering the questions in this section will help you to clarify the purpose of the investigation. By asking you the reasons for specific steps in the Procedure, this section prepares you to carry out the Laboratory Investigation. Questions in this section may also highlight safety concerns to which you should pay careful attention.

Materials A list of all required materials appears at the beginning of the investigation.

The quantity of material for each investigation is indicated for individual students, pairs of students, or groups of students.

Safety The Safety section warns you of potential hazards and tells you about precautions you should take to decrease the risk of accidents. The safety symbols that are relevant to the Laboratory Investigation appear next to the title of the Safety section. They also appear next to certain steps of the Procedure.

Procedure This section provides detailed step-by-step instructions. Diagrams are included where necessary. The Procedure enables you to test the hypothesis.

Make sure you read the entire procedure carefully before you begin the investigation. Look for safety symbols and notes. If safety symbols appear next to a step in the Procedure, you should follow the corresponding safety precaution(s) for that step and all following steps. **CAUTION** statements within the steps of the Procedure warn of possible hazards. **Notes** in the Procedure provide special directions.

In keeping with scientific method, you will record your data by filling in data tables, graphing data, labeling diagrams, drawing observed structures, and answering questions.

Analysis and Conclusions Two steps of the scientific method—analyzing data and forming a conclusion—are represented in this section. Here, you are to analyze and interpret your experimental results. This section may also challenge you to apply your conclusions to real-life situations or related experiments.

Going Further This section suggests additional activities for you to pursue on your own. Some of these are extensions of the Laboratory Investigation. Others involve library research that you might perform with your teacher's permission.

Presenting Data

To seek answers to problems or questions they have about the world, scientists typically perform many experiments in the laboratory. In doing so, they observe physical characteristics and processes, select areas for study, and review the scientific literature to gain background information about the topic they are investigating. They then form hypotheses, test these hypotheses through controlled experiments, record and analyze data, and develop a conclusion about the correctness of the hypotheses. Finally, they report their findings in detail, giving enough information about their experimental procedure so that other scientists are able to replicate the experiments and verify the results.

The Laboratory Investigations in *Laboratory Manual B* provide an opportunity for you to investigate scientific problems in the same manner as that of a typical scientist. As you perform these investigations, you will employ many of the techniques and steps of the scientific method a working scientist does. Some of the most important skills you will acquire are associated with the step of the scientific method known as recording and analyzing data. Three of these skills are creating and filling in data tables, making drawings, and finding averages. Another set of skills useful in presenting data is examined in the Laboratory Skills activity titled Using Graphing Skills.

It is important to record data precisely—even if the results of an investigation appear to be wrong. And it is extremely important to keep in mind that developing laboratory skills and data analysis skills is actually more valuable than simply arriving at the correct answers. If you analyze your data correctly—even if the data are not perfect—you will be learning to think as a scientist thinks. And that is the purpose of this laboratory manual and your experience in the biology laboratory.

Data Tables

When scientists conduct various experiments and do research, they collect vast amounts of information: for example, measurements, descriptions, and other observations. To communicate and interpret this information, they must record it in an organized fashion. Scientists use data tables for this purpose.

You will be responsible for completing data tables for many of the Laboratory Investigations. Each column in a data table has a heading. The column headings explain where particular data are to be placed. The completed data tables will help you interpret the information you collected and answer the questions found at the end of each Laboratory Investigation.

Name_____ Class_____ Date _____

EXERCISE 1

Given the following information, complete Data Table 1. Then interpret the data and answer the five questions that follow.

Information: The following hair colors were found among three classes of students:

Class 1: brown—20   Class 2: brown—18   Class 3: brown—15
           black—1   black—0   black—4
           blond—4   blond—6   blond—15

Data Table

Hair Color	Class 1	Class 2	Class 3	Total
Brown				
Black				
Blond				

1. What type of information is being gathered?

   _____

   _____

2. Which hair color occurs most often?

   _____

   _____

3. From the information in the Data Table, can you give the number of boys with black hair?

   _____

4. What information can you give about the number of students with black hair?

   _____

5. Which class has the most blond students?

   _____

   _____

6. How many students made up the entire student population?

   _____

   _____

EXERCISE 2

Given the following information, organize the data into a table. Use the blank area provided in Figure 1 to draw in the necessary columns and rows. Then interpret the data and answer the questions that follow.

Information: On an expedition around the world, several scientists collected the venom of various snakes. One of the tests that the scientists conducted determined the toxicity of the venom of each snake. Other data obtained by the scientists included the mortality percentage, or relative death rate, from the bites of various snakes.

The snakes observed were the (1) southern United States copperhead, (2) western diamondback rattlesnake, (3) eastern coral snake, (4) king cobra, (5) Indian krait, (6) European viper, (7) bushmaster, (8) fer-de-lance, (9) black-necked cobra, (10) puff adder.

The mortality percentage of people bitten by the snakes varied from 100% to less than 1%. The scientists noted the mortality percentage for each of the snakes was (1) less than 1%, (2) 5–15%, (3) 5–20%, (4) greater than 40%, (5) 77%, (6) 1–5%, (7) usually 100%, (8) 10–20%, (9) 11–40%, and (10) 11–40%.

Figure 1

1. Which snake's venom has the highest mortality rate?

_____

2. Which snake's venom has the lowest mortality rate?

_____

3. From the information recorded, can you determine the snake whose venom works the most rapidly? The least rapidly?

_____

4. Which two snakes' venom have the same mortality rate?

_____

5. How many types of snakes were observed?

_____

DRAWINGS

Laboratory drawings can be made using several methods. Some drawings are made in circles that represent the viewing field of a microscope or another type of magnifier. When completing these drawings, be sure to include the magnification at which you viewed the object. Other laboratory drawings represent organisms or parts of organisms. These drawings show the relative size, shape, and location of anatomical structures. When completing representative drawings, make the structures as clear and as accurate as possible.

Most laboratory drawings are labeled. Use the following guidelines to help make your laboratory drawings clear and legible.

- Use a ruler to draw label lines.
- Label lines should point to the center of the structure being labeled.
- Do not write on the label lines.
- Print all labels horizontally.
- Label the right-hand side of the drawing, if possible.
- Do not cross label lines.

EXERCISE 3

The following drawing was made without using the guidelines above. Circle those parts of the drawing that do not follow the guidelines. Then, on the lines provided, explain how the drawing should be done.

Magnification _____

Onion Cells

Figure 2

AVERAGES

Occasionally you will be required to find the average of data gathered from an investigation. To find an average, add the items in the group together and then divide the total by the number of items. For example, if there were five students of different ages—12, 13, 14, 17, and 19—how would you find the average age of the group? Add the five ages together and divide the total by 5, which is the number of items (students) in the group. What is the average age of this group of students? Your answer should be 15 years old.

EXERCISE 4

In a garden the heights of six sunflowers are 135.0 cm, 162.5 cm, 180.0 cm, 235.0 cm, 185.0 cm, and 167.5 cm. What is the average height of the sunflowers?

_____

EXERCISE 5

Find the average for the following group of data. Then use the results to answer the questions that follow.

In an experiment on plant growth and overcrowding, plants of the following heights are in three equal-sized containers.

Flowerpot 1:   20.0 cm and 18.2 cm
Flowerpot 2:   12.0 cm, 10.8 cm, 11.2 cm, and 12.4 cm
Flowerpot 3:   7.5 cm, 8.0 cm, 6.0 cm, 6.2 cm, 5.8 cm, and 7.3 cm

1. What is the average height of the plants in each flowerpot?

_____

_____

2. In which flowerpot did the plants grow the tallest? Explain.

_____

_____

EXERCISE 6

Find the averages for the following groups of data. Express your answers to the nearest tenth.

In a sample group of students, the number of breaths per minute was measured at rest and after exercise. The results were as follows:

At rest
Males: 10.1, 13.0, 12.5, 10.2, 13.1, 11.8
Females: 10.4, 13.0, 12.1, 11.9, 10.5, 12.8

After exercise
Males: 18.9, 23.7, 22.6, 21.3, 19.2, 20.6
Females: 25.0, 26.7, 29.0, 35.3, 33.1, 31.7

1. What is the average number of breaths per minute for males at rest? _____
   Females at rest? _____
2. What is the average number of breaths per minute for males after exercise? _____
   Females after exercise? _____
3. How many students make up the sample group? _____
4. What is the average number of breaths per minute for the entire group at rest? _____
   After exercise? _____
5. Do males or females take more breaths per minute at rest? _____
   After exercise? _____

Recognizing Laboratory Safety

Introduction

An important part of your study of biology will be working in a laboratory. In the laboratory, you and your classmates will learn biology by actively conducting and observing experiments. Working directly with living things will provide opportunities for you to better understand the principles of biology discussed in your textbook or talked about in class.

Most of the laboratory work you will do is quite safe. However, some laboratory equipment, chemicals, and specimens can be dangerous if handled improperly. Laboratory accidents do not just happen. They are caused by carelessness, improper handling of equipment and specimens, or inappropriate behavior.

In this investigation, you will learn how to prevent accidents and thus work safely in a laboratory. You will review some safety guidelines and become acquainted with the location and proper use of safety equipment in your classroom laboratory.

Problem

What are the proper practices for working safely in a biology laboratory?

Pre-Lab Discussion

Read the entire investigation. Then, work with a partner to answer the following questions.

1. Why might eating or drinking in the laboratory be dangerous?

   _____

   _____

   _____

2. How can reading through the entire investigation before beginning the Procedure help prevent accidents?

   _____

   _____

   _____

3. Look around the room. What safety equipment do you recognize?

   _____

4. What safety procedures should you follow when cleaning up at the end of an investigation?

   _____

5. Can minor safety procedures be skipped in order to finish the investigation before the bell rings?

   _____

Materials *(per group)*

Biology textbook

Laboratory safety equipment (for demonstration)

Procedure

1. Carefully read the list of laboratory safety rules listed in Appendix B of your textbook.

2. Special symbols are used throughout this laboratory manual to call attention to investigations that require extra caution. Use Appendix B in your textbook as a reference to describe what each symbol printed below means, or refer to the list of safety symbols on page 8 of this book.

1. _____
   _____

2. _____
   _____

3. _____
   _____

4. _____
   _____

5. _____
   _____

6. _____
   _____

7. _____
   _____

8. _____
   _____

3. Your teacher will point out the location of the safety equipment in your classroom laboratory. Pay special attention to instructions for using such equipment as fire extinguishers, eyewash fountains, fire blankets, safety showers, and items in first-aid kits. Use the space provided below to list the location of all safety equipment in your laboratory.

_____

_____

_____

_____

_____

Analysis and Conclusions

Observing Look at each of the following drawings and explain why the laboratory activities pictured are unsafe.

1. _____

_____

_____

_____

_____

_____

_____

_____

2. _____

_____

_____

_____

_____

_____

_____

_____

_____

3. _____

_____

_____

_____

_____

_____

_____

4. _____

Going Further

Many houseplants and some plants found in biology laboratories are poisonous. Use appropriate library resources to do research on several common poisonous plants. Share your research with your classmates. You may prepare a booklet describing common poisonous plants. Use drawings or photographs to illustrate your booklet.

Making Metric Measurements

Introduction

In many biology investigations, precise measurements must be made before observations can be interpreted. For everyday measuring, we still use English units such as the inch, quart, and pound. For scientific work, and for everyday measuring in most countries, the International System of Units (SI) is used. Eventually our country will use SI units for everyday measuring too.

Like our money system, SI is a metric system. All units are based on the number 10. In the SI system it is easy to change one unit to another because all units are related to one another by a power of 10.

In this investigation, you will review SI units for measuring length, liquid volume, and mass. You will also learn how to use some common laboratory equipment used for measuring.

Problem

How are metric units of measurement used in the laboratory?

Pre-Lab Discussion

Read the entire investigation. Then, work with a partner to answer the following questions.

1. Why do scientists and other people in most countries use the metric system for measurements?

_____

_____

2. Why is it easy to change from one unit to another in the SI system?

_____

3. What connections can you identify between the metric units for length and volume?

_____

_____

_____

_____

4. Why is it difficult to convert miles to yards or feet?

_____

_____

5. Name several aspects of everyday life that will change when our country converts to SI units.

_____

_____

Materials *(per group)*

meter stick

metric ruler

small test tube

rubber stopper

coin

triple-beam balance

50-mL beaker

100-mL graduated cylinder

Safety 🔧🧤

Handle all glassware carefully. Note all safety alert symbols next to the steps in the Procedure and review the meaning of each symbol by referring to Safety Symbols on page 8.

Procedure

Part A. Measuring Length

1. Use the meter stick to measure the length, width, and height of your laboratory table or desk in meters. Record your measurements to the nearest hundredth of a meter in Data Table 1.

2. Convert the measurements from meters to centimeters and then to millimeters. Record these measurements in Data Table 1.

3. Use a metric ruler to measure the length of a small test tube and the diameter of its mouth in centimeters. Record your measurements to the nearest millimeter in Data Table 2.

4. Convert the measurements from centimeters to millimeters. Record these measurements in Data Table 2.

Data Table 1

Lab Table Measurements			
Dimension	m	cm	mm
Length			
Width			
Height			

Data Table 2

Test Tube Measurements		
Dimension	cm	mm
Length		
Diameter of mouth		

Part B. Measuring the Volume of a Liquid

1. Fill the test tube to the top with water. Pour the water into the graduated cylinder.

2. The surface of the liquid will be slightly curved. This curved surface is called a meniscus. To measure the volume accurately, your eye must be at the same level as the bottom of the meniscus. See Figure 1. Record the volume of the water from the test tube to the nearest milliliter in Data Table 3.

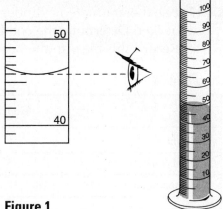

Figure 1

Data Table 3

Measurement of Volume	
Object	Volume (mL)
Water in test tube	

Part C. Measuring Mass

1. Place the 50-mL beaker on the pan of the balance. Be sure that the riders on the triple-beam balance are moved all the way to the left and that the pointer rests on zero. See Figure 2.

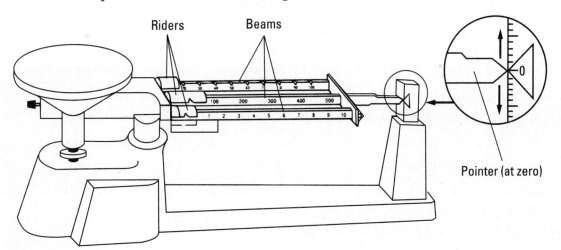

Figure 2

2. Move the rider on the middle beam to the right one notch at a time until the pointer drops below zero. Move the rider left one notch.

3. Move the rider on the back beam one notch at a time until the pointer again drops below zero. Move the rider left one notch.

4. Slide the rider along the front beam until the pointer stops at zero. The mass of the object is equal to the sum of the readings on the three beams.

5. Record the mass of the beaker to the nearest tenth of a gram in Data Table 4 on p. 30. Remove the beaker.

6. Repeat steps 2 through 5 using the rubber stopper and then the coin.

7. Use the graduated cylinder to place exactly 40 mL of water in the beaker. Determine the combined mass of the beaker and water. Record this mass to the nearest tenth of a gram in Data Table 4.

Data Table 4

Measurement of Mass	
Object	**Mass (g)**
50-mL beaker	
Rubber stopper	
Coin	
50-mL beaker plus 40 mL of water	

Analysis and Conclusions

1. Calculating How do you convert meters to centimeters? Centimeters to millimeters?

_____

2. Observing What is the largest volume of liquid your graduated cylinder can measure?

_____

3. Observing What is the smallest volume of a liquid your graduated cylinder can measure?

_____

4. Calculating What is the largest mass of an object your balance can measure?

_____

5. Observing What is the smallest mass of an object your balance can measure?

_____

6. Calculating What is the mass of 40 mL of water?

_____

7. Predicting How would you find the mass of a certain amount of water that you poured into a paper cup?

_____

_____

8. Calculating In this investigation you found the mass of 40 mL of water. Based on your observations, what is the mass of 1 mL of water?

_____

Going Further

If other types of laboratory balances are available, such as an electronic balance or a double-pan balance, use them to find the masses of several different objects. Compare the accuracy of the different balances.

Applying the Scientific Method

Introduction

The scientific method is a procedure used to gather information and test ideas. Scientists use the scientific method to answer questions about life and living organisms. Experimentation is an important part of the scientific method. In order to ensure that the results of an experiment are due to the variable being tested, a scientist must have both an experimental setup and a control setup. The experimental setup and the control setup differ only in the variable being tested.

In this investigation, you will form a hypothesis, test it, and draw a conclusion based on your observations.

Problem

Is light necessary for the sprouting of a potato?

Pre-Lab Discussion

Read the entire investigation. Then, work with a partner to answer the following questions.

1. Under what conditions do potatoes usually grow?

_____

2. Why is it important to seal the plastic bags?

_____

3. How does cutting one potato in half help limit the variables of the experiment?

_____

_____

4. Why is it necessary to keep both potato halves on moist paper towels?

_____

5. What evidence will tell you whether or not light is necessary for sprouting a potato?

_____

Materials (per group)

1 medium-sized potato
2 plastic bags with twist ties
knife
2 paper towels

Safety 🧍✂️

Put on a laboratory apron. Be careful when handling sharp instruments. Note all safety alert symbols next to the steps in the Procedure and review the meaning of each symbol by referring to Safety Symbols on page 8.

Procedure

1. With the members of your group, discuss whether or not the potato needs light to sprout. Based on your discussion, record your hypothesis in the space provided.
Hypothesis:

_____

_____

✂️ 2. Carefully cut the potato in half lengthwise. Count the number of eyes on the potato half to be put in the dark and on the half to be put in the light. Record this information in the Data Table.

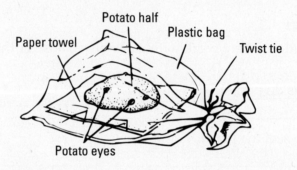

Potato half
Paper towel
Plastic bag
Twist tie
Potato eyes

Figure 1

3. Fold each paper towel repeatedly until you have a rectangle about the same size as your potato halves. Moisten the towels with water. Place a folded paper towel in each plastic bag.

4. Place a potato half in each plastic bag with the cut surface on the paper towel. Tie each bag with a twist tie. See Figure 1.

5. Place one of the plastic bags in a place that receives light. Place the other plastic bag in a dark place. Be sure that the potato halves remain on top of the paper towels and that both potato halves are kept at the same temperature.

6. After one week, open each plastic bag and count the number of sprouts. Record this information in the Data Table.

7. To calculate the percentage of eyes sprouting, divide the number of sprouts by the number of eyes and multiply the result by 100. Record your answers in the Data Table.

8. Have one person from your group go to the chalkboard to record your group's data in the table that has been drawn by your teacher.

Name_____ Class_____ Date _____

Data Table

	Number of Eyes	Number of Sprouts	Percentage of Eyes Sprouting
Potato half in dark			
Potato half in light			

Analysis and Conclusions

1. **Observing** Did more sprouts grow in the light or in the dark?

_____

2. **Controlling Variables** What was the control setup in this investigation?

_____

_____

3. **Controlling Variables** What was the experimental setup in this investigation?

_____

4. **Drawing Conclusions** What conclusion can you draw from this investigation?

_____

5. **Evaluating and Revising** How does your hypothesis compare with your results after completing the investigation?

_____

_____

_____

6. **Controlling Variables** Why was it important to keep both the control setup and the experimental setup at the same temperature throughout the experiment?

_____

_____

_____

Going Further

Devise an experiment to see if another variable, such as temperature or water, affects the number of sprouts a potato produces.

Using a Compound Light Microscope

Introduction

Many objects are too small to be seen by the eye alone. They can be seen, however, with the use of an instrument that magnifies, or visually enlarges, the object. One such instrument, which is of great importance to biologists and other scientists, is the compound light microscope. A compound light microscope consists of a light source or mirror that illuminates the object to be observed, an objective lens that magnifies the image of the object, and an eyepiece (ocular lens) that further magnifies the image of the object and projects it into the viewer's eye.

Objects, or specimens, to be observed under a microscope are generally prepared in one of two ways. Prepared or permanent slides are made to last a long time. They are usually purchased from biological supply houses. Temporary or wet-mount slides are made to last only a short time—usually one laboratory period.

The microscope is an expensive precision instrument that requires special care and handling. In this investigation, you will learn the parts of a compound light microscope, the functions of those parts, and the proper use and care of the microscope. You will also learn the technique of preparing wet-mount slides.

Problem

What is the proper use of a compound light microscope?

Pre-Lab Discussion

Read the entire investigation. Then, work with a partner to answer the following questions.

1. Why might it be a good idea to keep your microscope at least 10 cm from the edge of the table?

_____

2. Why should a microscope slide and coverslip be held by their edges?

_____

_____

3. Why do scientists use microscopes?

_____

4. Why should you use lens paper only once?

_____

_____

5. Why is it important to eliminate air bubbles from the slide?

_____

Materials *(per group)*

compound light microscope
prepared slide
lens paper
soft cloth (or cheesecloth)
newspaper

microscope slide
coverslip
dissecting probe
dropper pipette
scissors

Safety 🔬🧤♨️🥼

Put on a laboratory apron. Always handle the microscope with extreme care. You are responsible for its proper care and use. Use caution when handling microscope slides, as they can break easily and cut you. Never use direct sunlight as a light source for a compound light microscope. The sunlight reflecting through the microscope could damage your eye. Be careful when handling sharp instruments. Observe proper laboratory procedures when using electrical equipment. Note all safety alert symbols next to the steps in the Procedure and review the meaning of each symbol by referring to Safety Symbols on page 8.

Procedure

Part A. Care of the Compound Light Microscope

1. Figure 1 shows the proper way to carry a microscope. Always carry the microscope with both hands. Grasp the arm of the microscope with one hand and place your other hand under the base. Always hold the microscope in an upright position so that the eyepiece cannot fall out. Place a microscope on your worktable or desk at least 10 cm from the edge. Position the microscope with the arm facing you.

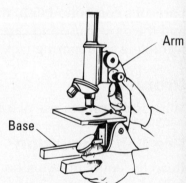

Arm

Base

Figure 1

2. Notice the numbers etched on the objectives and on the eyepiece. Each number is followed by an "X" that means "times." For example, the low-power objective may have the number "10X" on its side, as shown in Figure 2. That objective magnifies an object 10 times its normal size. Record the magnifications of your microscope in the Data Table. The total magnification of a microscope is calculated by multiplying the magnification of the objective by the magnification of the eyepiece. For example:

magnification of objective	×	magnification of eyepiece	=	total magnification
10X	×	10X	=	100X

Use the formula to complete the Data Table.

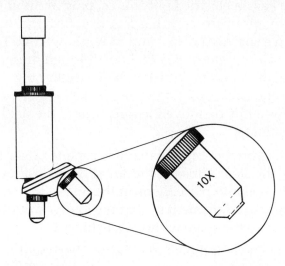

Figure 2

Data Table

Objective	Magnification of Objective	Magnification of Eyepiece	Total Magnification
Low power			
High power			
Other			

4. Before you use the microscope, clean the lenses of the objectives and eyepiece with lens paper. **Note:** *To avoid scratching the lenses, never clean or wipe them with anything other than lens paper. Use a new piece of lens paper on each lens you clean. Never touch a lens with your finger. The oils on your skin may attract dust or lint that could scratch the lens.*

Part B. Use of a Compound Light Microscope

1. Look at the microscope from the side. Locate the coarse adjustment knob that moves the objectives up and down. Practice moving the coarse adjustment knob to see how it moves the objectives with each turn.

2. Turn the coarse adjustment so that the low-power objective is positioned about 3 cm from the stage. Locate the revolving nosepiece. Turn the nosepiece until you hear the high-power objective click into position. See Figure 3. When an objective clicks into position, it is in the proper alignment for light to pass from the light source through the objective into the viewer's eye. Now turn the nosepiece until the low-power objective clicks back into position. **Note:** *Always look at the microscope from the side when moving an objective so that the microscope does not hit or damage the slide.*

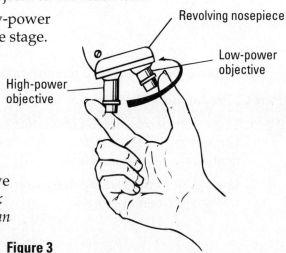

Revolving nosepiece

Low-power objective

High-power objective

Figure 3

3. If your microscope has an electric light source, plug in the cord and turn on the light. If your microscope has a mirror, turn the mirror toward a light source such as a desk lamp or window. **CAUTION:** *Never use the sun as a direct source of light.* Look through the eyepiece. Adjust the diaphragm to permit sufficient light to enter the microscope. The white circle of light you see is the field of view. If your microscope has a mirror, move the mirror until the field of view is evenly illuminated.

4. Place a prepared slide on the stage so that it is centered over the stage opening. Use the stage clips to hold the slide in position. Turn the low-power objective into place. Look at the microscope from the side and turn the coarse adjustment so that the low-power objective is as close as possible to the stage without touching it.

5. Look through the eyepiece and turn the coarse adjustment to move the low-power objective away from the stage until the object comes into focus. To avoid eyestrain, keep both eyes open while looking through a microscope. **CAUTION:** *To avoid moving the objective into the slide, never lower the objective toward the stage while looking through the eyepiece.*

6. Turn the fine adjustment to bring the object into sharp focus. You may wish to adjust the diaphragm so that you can see the object more clearly. In the appropriate space below, draw what you see through the microscope. Record the magnification.

7. Look at the microscope from the side and rotate the nosepiece until the high-power objective clicks into position. Look through the eyepiece. Turn the fine adjustment to bring the object on the slide into focus. **CAUTION:** *Never use the coarse adjustment when focusing the high-power objective lens. This could break your slide or damage the lens.* In the appropriate space below, draw what you see through the microscope. Record the magnification.

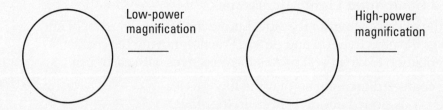

Low-power magnification _____

High-power magnification _____

8. Remove the slide. Move the low-power objective into position.

Part C. Preparing a Wet Mount

1. Use a pair of scissors to cut a letter "e" from a piece of newspaper. Cut out the smallest letter "e" you can find. Position the "e" on the center of a clean glass slide.

2. Use a dropper pipette to place one drop of water on the cut piece of newspaper. See Figure 4B.

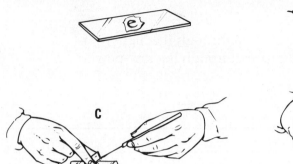

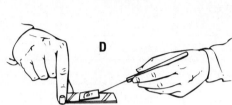

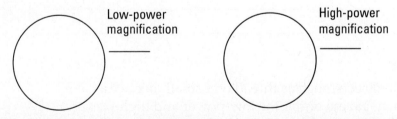

Figure 4

 3. Hold a clean coverslip in your fingers as shown in Figure 4C. Make sure the bottom edge of the coverslip is in the drop of water. Use a dissecting probe to slowly lower the coverslip onto the wet newspaper. Slowly lowering the coverslip prevents air bubbles from being trapped between the slide and the coverslip. The type of slide you have just made is called a wet mount. Practice making a wet mount until you can do so without trapping air bubbles on the slide.

4. Center the wet mount on the stage with the letter "e" in its normal upright position. **Note:** *Make sure the bottom of the slide is dry before you place it on the stage.* Turn the low-power objective into position and bring the "e" into focus. In the appropriate place below, draw the letter "e" as seen through the microscope. Record the magnification.

5. While looking through the eyepiece, move the slide to the left. Notice the way the letter seems to move. Now move the slide to the right. Again notice the way the letter seems to move. Move the slide up and down and observe the direction the letter moves.

6. Turn the high-power objective into position and bring the letter "e" into focus. In the appropriate place below, draw the letter "e" as seen through the microscope. Record the magnification.

Low-power magnification ____

High-power magnification ____

7. Take apart the wet mount. Clean the slide and coverslip with soap and water. Carefully dry the slide and coverslip with paper towels and return them to their boxes.

8. Rotate the low-power objective into position and use the coarse adjustment to place it as close to the stage as possible without touching. Carefully pick up the microscope and return it to its storage area.

Analysis and Conclusions

1. **Inferring** Why do you place one hand under the base of the microscope as you carry it?

_____

2. **Observing** How is the image of an object seen through the high-power objective different from the image seen through the low-power objective?

_____

_____

_____

3. **Observing** How does the letter "e" as seen through the microscope differ from the way an "e" normally appears?

_____

_____

4. **Inferring** Explain why a specimen to be viewed under the microscope must be thin.

_____

_____

_____

5. **Inferring** Why should you never use coarse adjustment when focusing the high-power objective lens?

_____

_____

6. **Drawing Conclusions** Suppose you were observing an organism through the microscope and noticed that it moved toward the bottom of the slide and then it moved to the right. What does this tell you about the actual movement of the organism?

_____

_____

_____

_____

Going Further

View some common objects, such as thread or a small piece of a color photograph from a magazine under the low-power and high-power objectives of the microscope. Make a drawing for each object. Describe the appearance of the objects when viewed under a microscope.

Laboratory Skills 6

Using a Bunsen Burner

Introduction

Sometimes a biologist needs to heat materials. In the laboratory, one of the most efficient ways to do this is to use a Bunsen burner. Bunsen burners are made in a variety of designs. In every one, however, a mixture of air and gas is burned. In most Bunsen burners, the amounts of air and gas can be controlled. In some laboratories, electric hot plates or portable gas burners are used instead of Bunsen burners.

In this investigation, you will learn the parts of the Bunsen burner and their functions. You will also learn how to use the Bunsen burner safely in the laboratory.

Problem

How can the Bunsen burner be safely used to heat materials in the laboratory?

Pre-Lab Discussion

Read the entire investigation. Then, work with a partner to answer the following questions.

1. Why is it important to wear safety goggles when using a Bunsen burner?

_____

_____

2. Why is it important to tie back loose hair and clothing when using a Bunsen burner?

_____

_____

3. In addition to the items mentioned in questions 1 and 2, what other safety precautions should be followed before lighting a Bunsen burner?

_____

_____

_____

4. How is using a Bunsen burner different from using a candle?

_____

_____

_____

5. Why is it important to make sure that the volume of water and the starting temperature are the same in each trial?

_____

_____

Materials *(per group)*

Bunsen burner
ring stand
2 250-mL beakers
wire gauze
metric ruler

beaker tongs
iron ring
100-mL graduated cylinder
flint striker or matches
clock with second hand

Safety 🛡️🔥💧🔥

Put on a laboratory apron. Put on safety goggles. Handle all glassware carefully. Tie back loose hair and clothing when using the Bunsen burner. Use extreme care when working with heated equipment or materials to avoid burns. Note all safety alert symbols next to the steps in the Procedure and review the meaning of each symbol by referring to Safety Symbols on page 8.

Procedure

1. Examine your burner when it is *not* connected to the gas outlet. If your burner is the type that can easily be taken apart, unscrew the barrel from the base and locate the parts shown in Figure 1. As you examine the parts, think about their functions.

   • The barrel is the area where the air and gas mix.

   • The collar can be turned to adjust the intake of air. If you turn the collar so that the holes are larger, more air will be drawn into the barrel.

   • The air intake openings are the holes in the collar through which air is drawn in.

   • The base supports the burner so that it does not tip over.

   • The gas intake tube brings the supply of gas from the outlet to the burner.

   • The spud is the small opening through which the gas flows. The small opening causes the gas to enter with great speed.

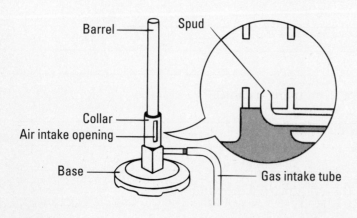

Figure 1

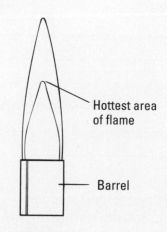

Figure 2

2. Reassemble the Bunsen burner if necessary and connect the gas intake tube to the gas outlet. **CAUTION:** *Put on safety goggles.* Make sure that the burner is placed away from flammable materials.

3. Adjust the collar so that the air intake openings are half open. If you use a match to light the burner, light the match and hold it about 2 cm above and just to the right of the barrel. Hold the match in this position while you open the gas outlet valve slowly until it is fully open. **CAUTION:** *To avoid burns on your hands, always use extreme care when handling lighted matches.* The burner can also be turned off by using the valve. Do not lean over the burner when lighting it.

4. If you use a flint striker to light the burner, hold the striker in the same position you would hold a lighted match. To light the burner with a striker, you must produce a spark at the same time you open the gas valve.

5. Practice lighting the burner several times. Every member of your group should be given the opportunity to light the burner.

6. The most efficient and hottest flame is blue in color and has distinct regions as shown in Figure 2. Adjust the collar so that the flame is blue and a pale blue inner cone is visible.

7. Adjust the flow of gas until the flame is about 6 cm high. Some burners have a valve in the base to regulate the flow of gas, but the flow of gas can always be adjusted at the gas outlet valve. After adjusting the flow of gas, shut off the burner. Leave your safety goggles on for the remainder of the investigation.

8. Arrange the apparatus as pictured in Figure 3.

9. Adjust the iron ring so that the bottom of the beaker is about 2 cm above the mouth of the burner barrel. Measure 100 mL of water in the graduated cylinder and pour it into one of the beakers.

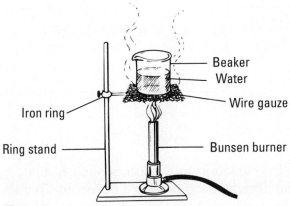

Beaker
Water
Wire gauze
Iron ring
Ring stand
Bunsen burner

Figure 3

10. Light the burner and heat the beaker of water. The bottom of the beaker should just be touching the top of the inner cone of the flame. In the Data Table on p. 44, record the time it takes for the water to start boiling rapidly. Using the beaker tongs, carefully remove the beaker and pour out the water.

11. Repeat steps 9 and 10 with the other beaker supported at a height of about 8 cm above the mouth of the barrel. **CAUTION:** *When raising the iron ring, use heat-resistant gloves.* In the Data Table, record the time it takes for the water to start boiling rapidly at this height. **Note:** *Be sure that the starting temperature of the water is the same in each trial.*

Data Table

Height Above Burner (cm)	Time to Boil (min)
2	
8	

Analysis and Conclusions

1. **Inferring** What would happen if the air intake openings were made very small?

_____

_____

2. **Drawing Conclusions** If the burner does not light after the gas outlet valve is opened, what might be wrong?

_____

3. **Observing** At what height, 2 cm or 8 cm, did the water come to a rapid boil faster?

_____

4. **Drawing Conclusions** Why is it necessary to know how to adjust the flow rates of the air and gas when using a Bunsen burner?

_____

_____

_____

5. **Controlling Variables** Why is it important to make sure that the volume of water and the starting temperature are the same in each trial?

_____

_____

Going Further

Test the ability of different kinds of laboratory burners, such as a hot plate, to heat water to boiling. Determine if there is a difference in the speed with which different burners are able to heat objects.

Preparing Laboratory Solutions

Introduction

A solution is a type of mixture in which one substance dissolves in another. In a solution, the substance that is dissolved is called the solute. The substance that does the dissolving is called the solvent. The most common solvent is water. Most solutions cannot easily be separated by simple physical means such as filtering.

Solutions in which water is the solvent, or aqueous solutions, are important to all types of living organisms. Marine microorganisms spend their entire lives in the ocean, an aqueous solution of water, salt, and other substances. Most of the nutrients needed by plants are in aqueous solution in moist soil. Plasma, the liquid part of the blood, is an aqueous solution containing dissolved nutrients and gases.

In this investigation, you will learn some of the techniques used to prepare laboratory solutions. You will also learn some of the proper uses of a triple-beam balance and a filtering apparatus.

Problem

What are some of the different ways in which laboratory solutions can be prepared?

Pre-Lab Discussion

Read the entire investigation. Then, work with a partner to answer the following questions.

1. What does the percentage concentration of a solution mean?

   _____

   _____

2. What is the difference between the mass/volume concentration of a solution and its volume/volume concentration?

   _____

   _____

3. Why is it difficult to dilute a solution accurately?

   _____

4. What is the relationship between a 30% sodium chloride solution and a 3% sodium chloride solution in terms of the number of solute molecules in each solution?

   _____

   _____

5. Why is a chemical placed on a piece of weighing paper instead of directly on the pan of a balance when its mass is being measured?

   _____

   _____

Materials *(per group)*

sodium chloride	weighing paper
10 mL of red food coloring	triple-beam balance
100-mL graduated cylinder	scoop
filter paper	10-mL graduated cylinder
funnel	ring stand
2 100-mL beakers	iron ring

Safety 🧪🧤🔪

Put on a laboratory apron. Put on safety goggles. Handle all glassware carefully. Always use special caution when working with laboratory chemicals, as they may irritate the skin or cause staining of the skin or clothing. Never touch or taste any chemical unless instructed to do so. Note all safety alert symbols next to the steps in the Procedure and review the meaning of each symbol by referring to Safety Symbols on page 8.

Procedure

Part A. Preparing the Mass/Volume Solution

1. To prepare a solution of a given percentage, dissolve the number of grams of solid solute equal to the percentage in enough water to make 100 mL of the solution. To prepare a 5% sodium chloride solution, place a piece of weighing paper on the pan of the triple-beam balance and find its mass.

2. Add exactly 5 g to the value of the mass of the weighing paper and move the riders of the balance to this number.

3. Using the scoop, add a small amount of sodium chloride at a time to the paper on the balance until the pointer rests on zero.

4. Add the 5 grams of sodium chloride to the 100-mL graduated cylinder.

5. Add enough water to bring the volume of the solution to 100 mL. What happens to the sodium chloride crystals?

_____

6. Dispose of this solution according to your teacher's instructions.

Part B. Preparing a Volume/Volume Solution

1. To prepare a solution of a given percentage, dissolve the number of milliliters of liquid solute equal to the percentage in enough solvent to make 100 mL of the solution. To prepare a 10% colored water solution, measure 10 mL of red food coloring in the 10-mL graduated cylinder and pour it into the large graduated cylinder. **CAUTION:** *Use caution with red food coloring to avoid staining your hands or clothing.*

2. Add enough water to the large graduated cylinder to bring the volume to 100 mL. What happens to the red food coloring as water is mixed with it?

_____

3. Keep this solution for use in Part C of this investigation.

Part C. Reducing the Concentration of a Solution

1. To reduce the concentration of a solution, pour the number of milliliters of the existing solution that is equal to the percentage of the new concentration into a graduated cylinder. Add enough solvent to bring the volume in milliliters to an amount equal to the percentage of the original solution. To reduce a 10% colored water solution to a 1% solution, pour the 10% colored water solution you prepared in Part B into a 100-mL beaker.

2. Measure 1 mL of the 10% solution in the 10-mL graduated cylinder.

3. Add enough water to the graduated cylinder to bring the volume to 10 mL. What differences do you observe between the 10% and 1% solutions of colored water?

_____

4. Dispose of the 1% solution according to your teacher's instructions. Keep the 10% solution for use in Part D of this investigation.

Part D. Filtering

1. Prepare a filter paper as shown in Figure 1. Fold a circle of filter paper across the middle. Fold the resulting half circle to form a quarter-circle. Open the folded paper into a cone, leaving the triple layer on one side and a single layer on the other.

2. Support a funnel as shown in Figure 2. Place the cone of the filter paper in the funnel and wet the paper so that it adheres smoothly to the walls of the funnel. Set a clean beaker beneath the funnel in such a way that the stem of the funnel touches the side of the beaker.

3. Pour the 10% colored water solution prepared in Part B slowly into the funnel. Do not let the mixture overflow the filter paper. As the mixture filters through the filter paper, record your observations in the Data Table on p. 48.

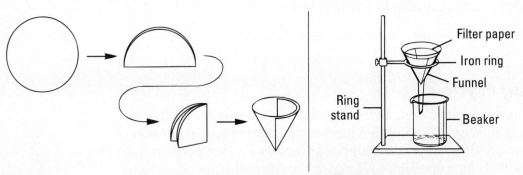

Figure 1   **Figure 2**

4. After all of the solution has passed through the filter paper into the beaker, observe the appearance of the filter paper. Record your observations in the Data Table.

5. Carefully remove the filter paper from the funnel and dispose of it and the colored water solution according to your teacher's instructions.

Data Table

Appearance of Liquid Before Filtering	Appearance of Liquid After Filtering	Appearance of Filter Paper After Filtering

Analysis and Conclusions

1. Comparing and Contrasting Relate the colors of the 10% and 1% colored water solutions to the number of solute molecules each solution contains.

_____

_____

2. Observing Was the filter paper successful in separating the two parts of the red food coloring solution? Use your observations to support your answer.

_____

_____

3. Communicating Results Describe the procedure needed to prepare a 30% sugar solution.

_____

_____

4. Communicating Results Describe the procedure needed to produce a 20% liquid bleach solution.

_____

5. Communicating Results Describe the procedure needed to reduce an 80% starch solution to a 20% solution.

_____

_____

Going Further

Solution concentrations can be expressed in a number of different ways, including molarity (the number of moles of solute per liter of solution) and molality (the number of moles of solute per kilogram of solvent). Using a chemistry reference text, describe the procedures used to prepare 1 molar and 1 molal concentrations.

Name______________________ Class______________ Date __________

Laboratory Skills 8

Using Graphing Skills

Introduction

Recorded data can be plotted on a graph. A graph is a pictorial representation of information recorded in a data table. It is used to show a relationship between two or more different factors. Two common types of graphs are line graphs and bar graphs.

In this investigation, you will interpret and construct a bar graph and a line graph.

Problem

How do you correctly interpret and construct a line graph and a bar graph?

Pre-Lab Discussion

Read the entire investigation. Then, work with a partner to answer the following questions.

1. Would a line graph or a bar graph be better for showing the number of birds of each color in a population?

____

2. How could you plot more than one responding variable on a line graph?

____

____

3. Where do you place the manipulated variable on a line graph?

____

4. Which type of graph would you use to show comparisons? Explain your reason.

____

5. Why is it important to have all parts of a graph clearly labeled and drawn?

____

Procedure

Part A. Interpreting Graphs

1. The type of graph that best shows the relationship between two variables is the line graph. A line graph has one or more lines connecting a series of points. See Figure 1. Along the horizontal axis, or x-axis, you will find the manipulated variable in the experiment. Along the vertical axis or y-axis, you will find the responding variable.

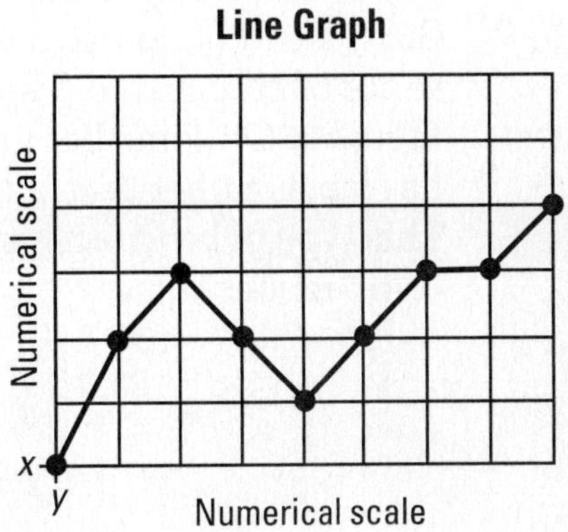
Line Graph
Numerical scale
Numerical scale
x
y

Figure 1

2. Use the line graph in Figure 2 to answer questions a through f below.

  a. Which plant grew the tallest? _____

  b. How many plants grew to be at least 6 cm tall? _____

  c. Which plant grew the fastest in the first five days? _____

  d. Which line represents plant 2? _____

  e. After 10 days, how much had plant 3 grown? _____

  f. How long did it take for plant 1 to grow 6 cm? _____

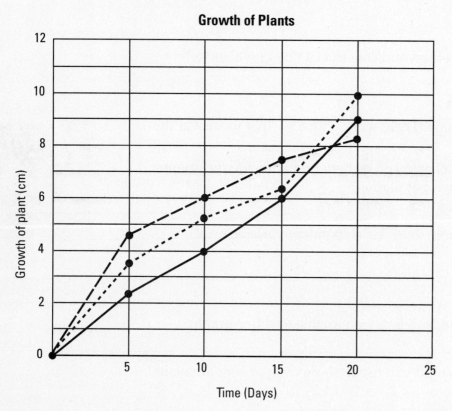

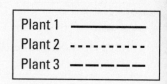

Figure 2

3. A bar graph is another way of showing relationships between variables. A bar graph also contains an x-axis and a y-axis. But instead of points, a bar graph uses a series of columns to display data. See Figure 3. On some bar graphs, the x-axis has labels rather than a numerical scale. This type of bar graph is used only to show comparisons.

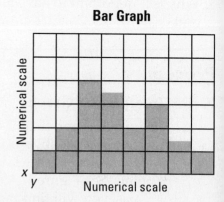

Figure 3

4. Use the bar graph in Figure 4 to answer questions a through e below.

    a. At birth, what is the average number of red blood cells per mm³ of blood?

_____

    b. What appears to happen to the number of red blood cells between birth and 2 months?

_____

    c. What happens to the number of red blood cells between the ages of 6 and 8 years?

_____

    d. Between what ages is a human likely to have 4.6 million red blood cells?

_____

    e. After 14 years of age, do males or females have a higher red blood cell count?

_____

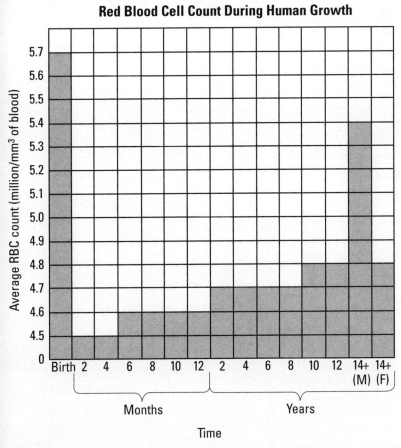

Figure 4

Part B. Constructing Graphs

1. When plotting data on a graph, you must decide which variable to place along the *x*-axis and which variable to place along the *y*-axis. Label the axes of your graph accordingly. Then you must decide on the scale of each axis; that is, how much each unit along the axis represents. Scales should be chosen to make the graph as large as possible within the limits of the paper and still include the largest item of data. If the scale unit is too large, your graph will be cramped into a small area and will be hard to read and interpret. If the scale unit is too small, the graph will run off the paper. Scale units should also be selected for ease of locating points on the graph. Multiples of 1, 2, 5, or 10 are easiest to work with.

2. Use the information recorded in Data Table 1 to construct a line graph on the grid provided below. You should label each axis, mark an appropriate scale on each axis, plot the data, connect the points, and give your graph a title.

Data Table 1

Temperature (°C)	Breathing Rate (per minute)
10	15
15	25
18	30
20	38
23	60
25	57
27	25

Breathing Rate of the Freshwater Sunfish

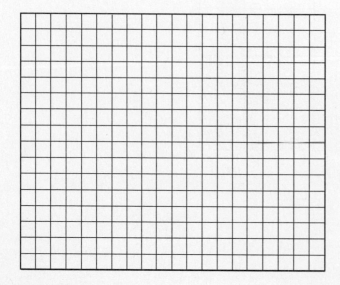

3. Use the information recorded in Data Table 2 to construct a bar graph on the grid provided below. You should label each axis, mark an appropriate scale on each axis, plot the data, darken the columns of the graph, and give your graph a title.

Data Table 2

Month	Jan.	Feb.	Mar.	April	May	June	July	Aug.	Sept.	Oct.	Nov.	Dec.
Rainfall (mL)	15	21	28	24	16	8	2	1	2	3	5	10

Average Rainfall in Willamette Valley

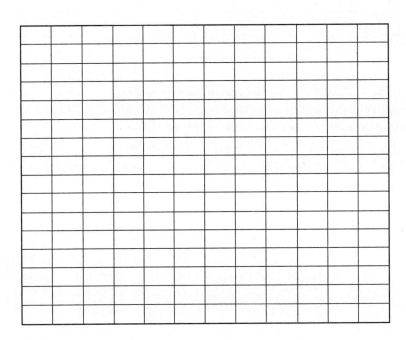

Analysis and Conclusions

1. Comparing and Contrasting How is a graph similar to a data table?

_____

_____

2. Comparing and Contrasting How is a line graph different from a bar graph?

_____

_____

3. Using Graphs Does a steep curve on a line graph indicate a rapid or slow rate of change?

_____

4. **Using Graphs** You are conducting an experiment to measure the gain in mass of a young mouse over a ten-week period. In constructing a graph to represent your data, which variable should you place along the *x*-axis and which variable should you place along the *y*-axis? Explain your answer.

_____

_____

_____

5. **Using Graphs** What is an advantage of using multiple lines in a line graph? (See Figure 2.)

_____

_____

_____

Going Further

A circle graph (sometimes called a "pie chart") is a convenient way to show the relative sizes of the parts that together form a whole body of data. Look through magazines and newspapers to find examples of circle graphs. Construct a chart listing the similarities and differences between circle graphs, line graphs, and bar graphs.

Chapter 1   The Science of Biology

Measuring Length, Mass, Volume, and Temperature

Introduction

Doing experiments is an important part of science. Most experiments include making measurements. Many different quantities can be measured. Some examples are length, mass, volume, temperature, and time. Some quantities, such as length, can be measured directly. Others, such as speed, are calculated from other measurements. In science you will probably use metric units to estimate, measure, and record data. The three fundamental metric units are the meter for length, the gram for mass, and the liter for capacity. In this investigation you will carry out different types of measurements.

Problem

What types of measurements are used to describe quantities?

Pre-Lab Discussion

Read the entire investigation. Then, work with a partner to answer the following questions.

1. Which of the measurements in the investigation are familiar to you? Which will be new to you?

   _____

2. How will you record a distance that is 2 centimeters longer than 5 meters? 2 centimeters shorter?

   _____

   _____

3. How will you choose an object to measure in millimeters?

   _____

   _____

4. Why would you measure the contents of a paper cup in milliliters (mL) rather than in liters?

   _____

   _____

   _____

5. Estimating quantities is a useful and practical skill. Describe a plan you can use to improve your ability to estimate quantities.

   _____

   _____

   _____

Materials *(per group)*

meter stick
millimeter ruler
250-mL graduated cylinder
laboratory balance and metric masses
thermometer
2 paper cups
30 cm of string
table-tennis ball
golf ball

Safety 🥽🧤🔥

Wear your lab apron and safety goggles at all times during this lab. Be careful not to break any glassware. Note all safety alert symbols next to the steps in the Procedure and review the meaning of each symbol by referring to Safety Symbols on page 8.

Procedure

🥽
🧤 **1.** Find an object whose length can be easily measured in centimeters. Make a sketch of the object in the space below. Then measure and record its length.

length: _____

2. Picture in your mind a familiar distance nearby that you think is 5 m long. Write a description of this distance below (for example, "The distance from our classroom to room 203 down the hall"). Then measure the distance with a meter stick and record your result. How good was your estimate?

_____

_____

_____

length: _____

3. Find an object whose width can be easily measured in millimeters. Make a sketch of the object in the space below. Then measure the object and record its length.

length: _____

4. Find a small object that fits easily on the pan of the balance scale. Make a sketch of the object in the space below, then find its mass in grams.

mass: _____

5. Fill a paper cup about two-thirds full with water. Pour the water into the graduated cylinder and record its volume in mL.
   CAUTION: *Be careful not to break glassware.*

   volume: _____

6. The volume of a rectangular solid is measured in cubic centimeters (cm^3). Find an object that is a rectangular solid. Then devise a way to find the volume of the object. What measurements will you need to make? Record each measurement and the volume of the object below.

   _____

   _____

   _____

   _____

   volume: _____

7. Fill a paper cup about two-thirds full with cool tap water. Place the thermometer in the water and find its temperature. Record your measurement below. Spill out the water. Now fill the cup with warm tap water. Use the thermometer to find the temperature of the water. Record your measurement.

   cool tap water: _____

   warm tap water: _____

8. Use the balance to find the mass of the golf ball. Record your measurement below. Then find and record the mass of the table-tennis ball.

   mass of golf ball: _____

   mass of table-tennis ball: _____

   Now take a piece of string and use it to measure the circumference of the golf ball at its widest point. You can do this by wrapping the string exactly once around the golf ball, then measuring the length of the string. Record your measurement below. Repeat this procedure for the table-tennis ball.

   circumference of golf ball: _____

   circumference of table-tennis ball: _____

Analysis and Conclusions

1. Comparing and Contrasting Which of the measurements did you find easiest to make? Which did you find most difficult? Why do you think so?

_____

_____

2. Comparing and Contrasting One student measured the height of a plant as 52 mm. Another student measured the same plant to the nearest tenth of a centimeter. What was the second student's measurement? Was one method more precise? Explain your answer.

_____

_____

3. Calculating A cube measuring 1 cm in each dimension holds 1 milliliter of water. Describe the dimensions of a cube that could hold 1 liter of water. What is the volume of this cube in cubic centimeters?

_____

_____

4. Measuring Why might two people measuring the same temperature get very different results?

_____

5. Inferring Why might it be a good practice to measure a quantity several times and average the results?

_____

_____

6. Comparing and Contrasting Look at the measurements that you recorded in step 8. In what way are these two balls similar? In what way are they quite different?

_____

_____

7. Forming Operational Definitions Describe a single measurement that would describe the similarity and difference that exists between the golf ball and table-tennis ball.

_____

Going Further

Find a local map that shows distances to the nearest tenth of a mile. Then have a friend with a car drive a short distance, such as 3 miles. Your friend should try to drive at a constant speed; for example, 30 miles per hour. Time the trip with a stop watch or watch with a second hand. Calculate the speed (distance divided by time) and compare the calculated speed with the speed shown on the car's speedometer. Do you think it is more accurate to calculate speed or to measure it? Give reasons for your opinion.

Discovering Where Proteins Are Found

Introduction

Your physical traits—from the shape of your ears to the color of your eyes—are determined by the proteins that are made in the cells of your body. Proteins are also present in the food you eat. Which foods contain proteins? In this investigation you will perform a simple experiment to find out.

Problem

How can you find out whether a food contains protein?

Pre-Lab Discussion

Read the entire investigation. Then, work with a partner to answer the following questions.

1. A chemical test using a substance called an indicator can be used to find out if a food contains protein. What indicator will you use in this investigation?

   _____

   _____

2. How will the indicator show you that protein is present in a food?

   _____

   _____

3. Can the indicator show that a food does *not* contain protein? If so, how?

   _____

   _____

4. What measuring tool will you use to measure 5 mL of the biuret reagent? What part of the instructions explains how to use this tool?

   _____

   _____

   _____

5. Why do the instructions in Step 3 tell you to put rubber stoppers in the test tubes?

   _____

   _____

Materials *(per group)*

5 test tubes
5 rubber stoppers
glass-marking pencil
test-tube rack
10-mL graduated cylinder
30-mL biuret reagent

egg white
cottage cheese
butter
canned tuna
milk
plastic gloves

Safety 🔬🥼🧤👁🔥

Wear your safety goggles and lab apron at all times during this lab. Be careful not to break any glassware. Always wear plastic gloves and use special caution when working with laboratory chemicals, as they may irritate the skin or stain skin or clothing. Never touch or taste any chemical unless instructed to do so. Wear plastic gloves when handling eggs or egg whites or tools that have been in contact with them. Wash hands thoroughly after carrying out this investigation. Note all safety alert symbols next to the steps in the Procedure and review the meaning of each symbol by referring to Safety Symbols on page 8.

Procedure

1. Place a small sample of each of the foods listed into a separate test tube. Use the glass-marking pencil to label each test tube.

2. Add 5 mL of biuret reagent to each test tube as shown in Figure 1. **CAUTION:** *Be careful not to spill biuret solution on your skin or clothing. If a spill occurs, rinse with plenty of water.*

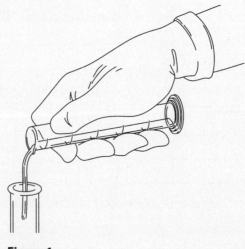

Figure 1

3. Seal each test tube with a rubber stopper. Shake each test tube and observe what happens. A pink or purple color indicates the presence of protein. If you do not see any color change, no protein is present. Record your observations in the Data Table.

Data Table

Food	Protein Present (Yes/No)
Egg white	
Cottage cheese	
Butter	
Tuna	
Milk	

Analysis and Conclusions

1. **Observing** Which foods contained protein?

_____

_____

2. **Classifying** How can your data table be used to classify the tested foods?

_____

3. **Designing Experiments** An iodine solution will change color if it is added to a food that contains starch. Design an experiment to determine if a food contains starch, protein, or both.

_____

_____

4. **Communicating Results** In this type of experiment, what is the meaning of a substance testing positive or negative?

_____

_____

_____

5. **Inferring** Labels on food usually state the number of grams of protein in one serving. Can biuret reagent be used to find out this information? Explain your reason.

_____

_____

6. **Evaluating and Revising** A student decided to repeat this experiment and include one more test tube. The student put distilled water in the sixth test tube. Why did the student change the experiment in this way?

_____

_____

Going Further

Do you think proteins are present in fruits, vegetables, and cereals? With your teacher's permission, design and perform an experiment to find out.

Investigating Chemical Cycles in the Biosphere

Introduction

Matter on Earth is constantly being recycled through living organisms and the nonliving environment. Several of these cycles are linked together.

During the process of photosynthesis, plants take in carbon dioxide and water and break down the molecules. Oxygen is released into the atmosphere, where it is used by living organisms for respiration. Two of the waste products of respiration are water and carbon dioxide. The carbon dioxide enters the atmosphere, where it can be used by plants in further photosynthesis. The water enters the atmosphere and later returns to the Earth as precipitation. This precipitation may become drinking water.

During this experiment, you will examine a portion of the oxygen cycle, the carbon cycle, and the water cycle in a closed environment.

Problem

How do carbon and oxygen cycle through the biosphere?

Pre-Lab Discussion

Read the entire investigation. Then, work with a partner to answer the following questions.

1. What is the purpose of Tube 4?

_____

_____

2. What is an indicator?

_____

_____

3. What will you record in the Data Table?

_____

_____

4. Why are the tubes sealed and not opened during the experiment?

_____

_____

5. Why is pond water used instead of tap water?

_____

_____

Materials *(per group)*

plastic gloves
2 snails
4 sprigs of water plants
pond water
masking tape
fluorescent plant lamp
bromthymol blue solution in dropper bottle
4 culture tubes with tops
test-tube rack

Safety

Put on a laboratory apron. Put on safety goggles. Be careful to avoid breakage when working with glassware. Always use special caution and wear disposable plastic gloves when working with laboratory chemicals, as they may irritate the skin or cause staining of the skin or clothing. Never touch or taste any chemical unless instructed to do so. Follow your teacher's directions and all appropriate safety procedures when handling live animals. Wash your hands well with soap and warm water before leaving the laboratory. Note all safety alert symbols next to the steps in the Procedure and review the meaning of each symbol by referring to Safety Symbols on page 8.

Procedure

1. Obtain four culture tubes with tops. Use tape to prepare four labels as shown in Figure 1. Place one label on each culture tube.
   CAUTION: *Wear your safety goggles and laboratory apron. Be careful not to break any glassware.*

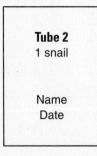 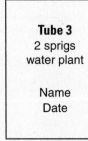 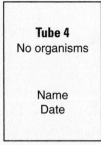

Tube 1	**Tube 2**	**Tube 3**	**Tube 4**
2 sprigs water plant and 1 snail	1 snail	2 sprigs water plant	No organisms
Name Date	Name Date	Name Date	Name Date

Figure 1

2. Into tube 1 place two sprigs of the water plant and one snail. Into tube 2 place one snail. Into tube 3 place two sprigs of the water plant.
   CAUTION: *Follow all safety precautions when handling plants and animals.*

3. Fill all four tubes with pond water. Add four drops of bromthymol blue solution to each tube. Seal each tube tightly. **CAUTION:** *Handle the bromthymol blue solution with care because it stains the skin and clothing. Wear plastic gloves.*

4. Set the tubes in a test-tube rack and place them near a bright light.

5. After 24 hours, observe the tubes. Notice whether the organisms are still alive. Note any color change in the water. Bromthymol blue solution is an indicator. In the presence of carbon dioxide, it changes color from blue to yellow. Record your observations in the Data Table.

6. Observe the tubes every day for seven days. Record your observations in the Data Table.

7. Empty all the tubes and dispose of the organisms according to your teacher's directions. Wash your hands with soap and warm water before leaving the laboratory.

Data Table

Observations				
Day	Tube 1	Tube 2	Tube 3	Tube 4
1				
2				
3				
4				
5				
6				
7				

Analysis and Conclusions

1. **Observing** What changes occured in the bromthymol blue solution in each tube?
   Tube 1

   _____

   _____

   Tube 2

   _____

   _____

   Tube 3

   _____

   _____

   Tube 4

   _____

   _____

2. **Inferring** At the end of seven days, what happened to the organism in tube 2? Why do you think this happened?

   _____

   _____

3. **Analyzing Data** Why did the organisms in tube 1 remain alive?

_____

_____

_____

4. **Inferring** Explain why the plants alone in tube 3 remained alive.

_____

_____

_____

5. **Drawing Conclusions** How does this investigation relate to the oxygen cycle?

_____

_____

6. **Drawing Conclusions** How does this investigation relate to the carbon dioxide cycle?

_____

_____

_____

7. **Drawing Conclusions** How does this investigation relate to the water cycle?

_____

_____

_____

8. **Predicting** What do you predict would happen if all of the tubes in the investigation were placed in the dark? Explain your prediction.

_____

_____

_____

Going Further

Repeat this investigation with different organisms or different combinations of organisms in each tube. You may also want to alter the size of the culture tubes or other containers. Be sure that all containers remain tightly sealed throughout the observation period. Report your observations and conclusions to the class.

Measuring the Effect of Bacteria on Plant Growth

Introduction

Ecologists often study the relationships among organisms living closely together. Different types of relationships exist. One organism may benefit while another is harmed, one may benefit while the other experiences no effect, or both may benefit. Bacteria live closely associated with other organisms. One particular type of bacterium, *Rhizobium*, infects the roots of plants. In this investigation, you will carry out a controlled experiment to determine whether the presence of *Rhizobium* affects bean plant growth.

Problem

How does the presence of *Rhizobium* bacteria affect the growth of plants?

Pre-Lab Discussion

Read the entire investigation. Then, work with a partner to answer the following questions.

1. Define the hypothesis that will be tested by your experiment.

   _____

   _____

   _____

   _____

2. What are the manipulated and responding variables in the experiment?

   _____

   _____

   _____

3. What is your control and what purpose will it serve?

   _____

   _____

4. Why do you think you are instructed to set up the "without" pot before the "with" pot?

   _____

   _____

5. Why is it important to give each pot the same amount of water?

   _____

   _____

   _____

Materials *(per group)*

two 5-inch plastic pots (sterile)
distilled or deionized water
legume seeds
horticultural vermiculite (less dusty) or perlite
plastic gloves
Rhizobium bacteria
plastic wrap
fluorescent plant lamp
nitrogen-free nutrients
metric ruler (centimeter markings)
laboratory balance (grams)

Safety 🖐🧤🚰🔥

Follow your teacher's directions and all appropriate safety procedures when handling microorganisms. Wash your hands well with soap after working with seeds, plants, or soil. Note all safety alert symbols next to the steps in the Procedure and review the meaning of each symbol by referring to Safety Symbols on page 8.

Procedure

 1. Working with a partner, label one pot "without" and one pot "with."

2. Fill each pot with an equal amount of vermiculite.

3. In the "without" pot, make three holes, evenly spaced, in the vermiculite. Your teacher will tell you how deep to make the holes. **Note:** *Make sure that you do not contaminate the "without" pot with bacteria.*

4. Place one seed in each of the three holes and cover with vermiculite. **CAUTION:** *Wear plastic gloves when working with laboratory chemicals and microorganisms.*

5. In the "with" pot, make three holes as in Step 3.

6. Inoculate three seeds with *Rhizobium* bacteria following your teacher's instructions.

7. Place one inoculated seed in each of three holes in the "with" pot.

8. Add distilled water to each pot slowly until water comes out of the drainage holes on the bottom of the pot.

9. Cover both of your pots with plastic wrap and put them in the place your teacher has indicated.

10. **Controlling Variables** Once germination occurs, water your plants as instructed by your teacher. **Note:** *It is important that each pot gets an equal amount of water.*

11. On the day of measuring, carefully remove the whole root mass from the pot. Shake it gently to remove the vermiculite.

12. Dip the roots up and down in a container of water until clean.

13. Measure the height of each plant to the nearest centimeter. **Note:** *Start where the roots attach to the stem and measure the distance to the top leaf.* Record the height in Data Table 1.

14. Place each plant on the balance and find the mass of each plant to the nearest gram. Record in Data Table 2.

15. Examine the roots of each plant closely and write down your observations in Data Table 1.

16. Find the average height and mass for each group of plants by finding the sum of all the heights and dividing by the total number of plants.

Data Table 1: Height

Plant Height (cm)	With *Rhizobium*	Without *Rhizobium*
Plant 1		
Plant 2		
Plant 3		
Average		
Observations of roots of plants		

Data Table 2: Mass

Plant Mass (g)	With *Rhizobium*	Without *Rhizobium*
Plant 1		
Plant 2		
Plant 3		
Average Mass		

Calculations

Height Difference = Average Height (cm) "With" − Average Height (cm) "Without"

Percentage Increase in Height = Difference / Average Height (cm) "Without" × 100

Mass Difference = Average Mass (g) "With" − Average Mass (g) "Without"

Percentage Increase in Mass = Difference / Average Mass (g) "Without" × 100

17. Dispose of all plant materials according to your teacher's directions. Wash your hands with soap and warm water before leaving the laboratory.

Analysis and Conclusions

1. **Analyzing Data** Was there a difference between the height and mass of the bean plants infected with bacteria and those that were not?

_____

_____

2. **Analyzing Data** What was the percentage increase in height and weight? Do you think the effect observed was significant? Explain your answer.

_____

_____

_____

_____

3. **Drawing Conclusions** Do the results support or contradict the hypothesis being tested? What conclusion can be drawn from the results? Explain.

_____

_____

_____

4. **Observing** What did you notice about the roots of the "with" plants that was different from the "without" plants? Why do you think this occurred?

_____

_____

_____

5. **Inferring** How would you characterize the type of interaction or relationship between the bacteria and the bean plant? Explain.

_____

_____

_____

_____

Going Further

What question(s) did the results of your experiment raise? Design an experiment that would address one such question or that would logically follow this experiment.

Think about the ultimate goal in growing beans. Is gathering data on height and weight as useful as investigating the number of fruits and seeds produced? How might an experiment be carried out to investigate the effect of *Rhizobium* on bean production?

Sampling a Plant Community

Introduction

A population is any group of the same species that lives in the same area. The number of individual organisms per unit of area is the population density of the area. In a crowded city where there are many apartments, the human population density is high. If you live in the country where houses are far apart, the human population density is low.

Scientists sometimes study an area of land to see how the living things there would be affected by a change, such as building on the land. To do this, scientists must first find out which species live in the area. Then they count the number of individuals in each species. This can tell them how many organisms may be disturbed by a change in the land.

It can be very difficult to count the organisms in a large area. So, scientists may find the populations in small parts of the large area. They then use the numbers from the smaller areas to estimate the population of the large area. This is called random sampling. In this investigation, you will use random sampling to estimate the population density of some plant species. You will also calculate what plants have the largest populations.

Problem

How can you estimate the size of a large population?

Pre-Lab Discussion

Read the entire investigation. Then, work with a partner to answer the following questions.

1. What will you do in steps 1 and 2 of this investigation?

   _____

2. How will you use the plant guidebooks in this investigation?

   _____

   _____

3. How will you choose a smaller area for counting species?

   _____

   _____

4. How many small squares will you make and count plants in within the large square?

   _____

5. How will counting plants in several small squares give you a better estimate of the total populations than counting plants in only one small square?

   _____

   _____

Materials *(per pair)*

protective work gloves

meter stick or metric tape measure

16 stakes

rubber mallet

large ball of string

scissors

plant guidebooks to woody and nonwoody plants

notepad for use in the field

right triangle (measuring tool)

Safety 🔪 ⬛ 🗱 ✋

Be careful when handling sharp instruments. Use the mallet and other tools carefully. You will be observing and handling plants outdoors. Alert your teacher in advance to any allergies you may have. To avoid possible contact with poisonous or prickly plants, wear work gloves. Use the plant guidebooks to identify dangerous plants. Do not disturb the nests of any animals you may encounter. Treat living organisms with respect. Return or dispose of all materials according to the instructions of your teacher. Note all safety alert symbols next to the steps in the Procedure and review the meaning of each symbol by referring to Safety Symbols on page 8.

Procedure

🔪 1. Work with a partner. As shown in Figure 1, use a tape measure or meter stick to measure off a square 10 m on a side. Then use the mallet to drive a stake into each of the four corners of the square. **CAUTION:** *Be careful not to injure yourself when using the mallet and stakes.*

🔪 2. Loop the string around the stakes to mark off the square. Cut the string and tie the ends together. **CAUTION:** *Be careful when handling sharp tools.*

🗱 3. Look at the plants in the square. Use plant guidebooks to help you
✋ find the names of the different species you see. Write the name of each species in Data Table 1. **CAUTION:** *Be aware of any poisonous or prickly plants. Be sure to wear work gloves.*

4. Now you will choose a smaller area in the square by closing your eyes and tossing an object into the square. Around the spot where the object lands, measure off a square 1 m on a side.

5. Use string and stakes to make the small square as shown in Figure 2. The right-triangle tool will help you make the corners square.

6. Look at the plants in the small square, as shown in Figure 3. Count the number of plants of each species and write their names and numbers in Columns 1 and 2 of Data Table 2.

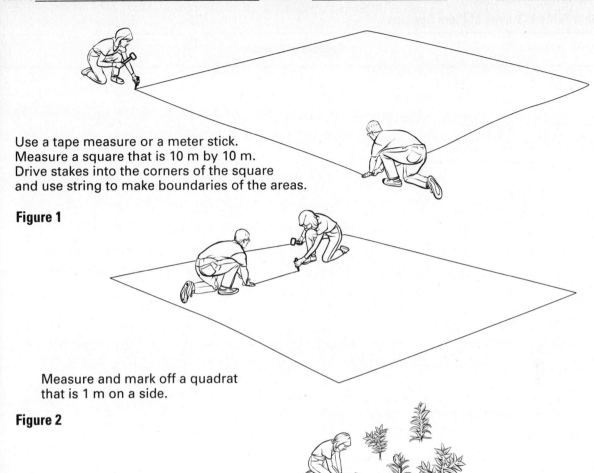

Use a tape measure or a meter stick.
Measure a square that is 10 m by 10 m.
Drive stakes into the corners of the square
and use string to make boundaries of the areas.

Figure 1

Measure and mark off a quadrat
that is 1 m on a side.

Figure 2

Use plant guidebooks to identify
the plants in the square.

Figure 3

7. Repeat steps 4 through 6 two more times, so you can count the
populations in two other small squares within the large square.
Write the numbers in Columns 3 and 4 of Data Table 2.

8. When you have finished identifying and counting the plants, pull
up the stakes, rewind the string, and return to class.

9. You now have a complete list of plant species and the number
counted in each of three small squares. Follow steps 10–12 below
to estimate the total population of each species in the large square.

10. First, find the total population of a species in the three squares by
adding the numbers across Columns 2, 3, and 4. Write the sum in
Column 5 of Data Table 2 on p. 74.

11. Now divide the number in Column 5 by 3 to find the average small
square population. Write this number in Column 6 of Data Table 2.

12. Multiply the average small square population in Column 6 by 100
to estimate the total population of the large square. Write this
number in Column 7 of Data Table 2.

Data Table 1: Survey of Plant Species

Species of Plants

Name_____ Class_____ Date _____

Data Table 2: Populations in Small Squares

Column 1	Column 2	Column 3	Column 4	Column 5	Column 6	Column 7
Species name	Number in small square 1	Number in small square 2	Number in small square 3	Total number in 3 squares	Average number per small square	Calculated total population in entire area, 10 m × 10 m

Analysis and Conclusions

1. **Analyzing Data** Look at Column 7 of Data Table 2. Which species has the smallest population in the large square area?

_____

_____

2. **Analyzing Data** Which species is the dominant species in the large square (the species with largest population)?

_____

_____

_____

3. **Comparing and Contrasting** Compare your results with other student teams in the class. Why do you think the population densities of some species were different from one part of the site to another? [**Hint:** Think about how differences in amounts of sunlight, type of ground, and availability of water may have had an effect.]

_____

_____

_____

_____

4. **Formulating Hypotheses** How might your large square change if human activity or disease destroyed the dominant species?

_____

_____

_____

_____

5. **Drawing Conclusions** Based on this investigation, do you think that counting random samples is good way to count a large population? Explain your answer.

_____

_____

_____

_____

Going Further

Think about how the population of one type of plant you counted might have been affected by a nonliving factor such as water or light. Plan an experiment to test your idea. If the necessary resources are available and you have your teacher's permission, perform the experiment.

Observing Decomposition

Introduction

More and more people are starting to put garbage in their gardens. You might think this practice would endanger health, smell bad, and damage the garden. But if it is done properly, it is safe, free of unpleasant odors, and beneficial to plant growth. Thanks to the action of helpful bacteria (which are often assisted by burrowing creatures such as worms), the garbage breaks down to form a dark-colored, nutrient-rich substance called compost. In this investigation, you will explore the process of making compost.

Problem

How can garbage be changed into compost?

Pre-Lab Discussion

Read the entire investigation. Then, work with a partner to answer the following questions.

1. Why can you assume that the decomposer bacteria need air in order to break down the materials in the bottle?

   _____

2. What else besides air do the bacteria need to make the compost?

   _____

3. Why can you infer that the bacteria causing unpleasant smells are harmed or killed by oxygen?

   _____

   _____

4. Why should you tell your teacher if the contents of the bottle start to become warm?

   _____

5. Do you think the height of the contents of the bottle will change over time? Explain your reason.

   _____

   _____

Materials *(per group)*

2-L clear plastic soda bottle	weeds and leaves	foam meat tray
small nail or push pin	uncooked vegetable	plastic gloves
scissors	and fruit scraps	
topsoil	glass-marking pencil	
150-mL beaker	cheesecloth	
scraps of paper	rubber band	
grass clippings	plastic fork	

Safety

Wear your goggles and laboratory apron at all times during this investigation. Use caution with the nail and scissors to avoid cutting yourself or others. Be careful to avoid breaking the glass beaker. Wear plastic disposable gloves and wash your hands well with soap after working with plant material, soil or compost. Note all safety alert symbols next to the steps in the Procedure and review the meaning of each symbol by referring to Safety Symbols on page 8.

Procedure

1. Carefully poke holes in the sides and bottom of the soda bottle with the nail. Use Figure 1 as a guide. **CAUTION:** *Be very careful and take your time.* Take turns making the holes—there are many to make.

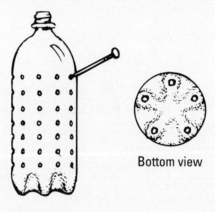

Bottom view

Figure 1

2. Using the nail, poke a large hole near the top of the bottle at the point where the sides become vertical and the plastic thins out. Starting this hole, carefully cut off the top of the bottle with the scissors as shown in Figure 2. **CAUTION:** *Be careful when working with sharp objects.*

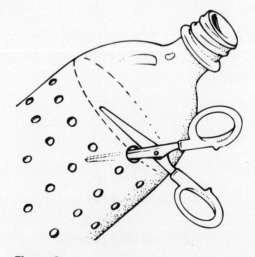

Figure 2

3. Label your bottle with the names of the people in your group and the date. Then put the bottle on the meat tray as shown in Figure 3A.

4. Fill the bottle about one-third full with grass clippings. Add 100 mL of soil, then 20 mL of water. The contents of the bottle should be moist but not soaking wet. If the contents are still dry, add a little more water. **CAUTION:** *Wear plastic gloves when handling plants. Be sure not to break any glassware.*

5. With the scissors, cut the paper, leaves, weeds, and vegetable and fruit scraps into pieces no larger than 1 cm across. Fill the bottle about one-half full with the cut-up materials.

6. Use the plastic fork to mix the contents of the bottle well. If any materials fall onto the meat tray, lift the bottle, remove the tray, and dump the tray's contents into the bottle. Then put the tray back under the bottle.

7. Make a mark on the outside of the bottle to indicate the height of the contents. Cover the bottle with a piece of cheesecloth. Secure the cheesecloth with the rubber band (see Figure 3B). Then place the bottle in a warm location. **CAUTION:** *Wash your hands well before leaving the laboratory.*

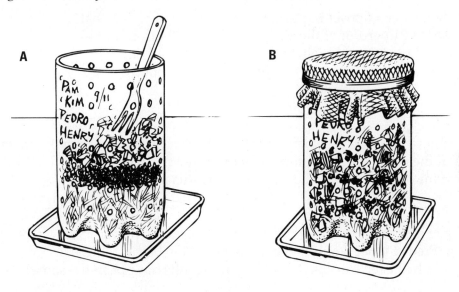

Figure 3

8. Twice a week, observe the contents of the bottle. Touch the sides of the bottle and note whether the bottle feels warm or cool to the touch. **CAUTION:** *If the bottle feels hot, notify your teacher immediately.*

9. After you have made your observations, add some water if the contents are dry. Once a week, mix the contents with the fork and mark their height on the side of the bottle. Write the date next to the new mark. Make sure you replace the cheesecloth when you have finished making your observations. **Note:** *If the contents start to smell bad, like rotten eggs or vinegar, mix the contents every time you make your observations.*

Analysis and Conclusions

1. **Observing** How did the contents of the bottle change over time?

_____

_____

_____

2. **Observing** How did the level of the bottle's contents change over time?

_____

_____

3. **Observing** How long did it take for the contents of the bottle to finish decomposing?

_____

4. **Observing** What does your "finished" compost look like?

_____

_____

5. **Inferring** How did the materials in the bottle change?

_____

_____

6. **Inferring** Some decomposer bacteria use oxygen, a substance that makes up about 21 percent of the air you breathe. Others do not use oxygen, but are not harmed by it. Still others are slowed down or even killed by oxygen. What can you infer about decomposer bacteria and making compost?

_____

_____

7. **Inferring** If the materials in a compost heap are not mixed regularly, it may start to smell bad. Explain why this might occur.

_____

_____

8. **Predicting** Predict what would have happened if the bottle and the materials in it had been sterilized. Would your results have been the same?

_____

_____

Going Further

Design an experiment to test how the formation of compost is affected by one of the following factors: light, heat, moisture, air.

Investigating Cells, Tissues, and Organs

Introduction

In addition to providing us with nutritious food, chicken eggs and meat also provide us with the opportunity for firsthand examination of cells, tissues, and organs. The structure and function of chicken muscles, bones, liver, heart, and skin are similar in many respects to those of humans.

In this investigation you will examine the structure and function of various cells, tissues, and organs in the chicken.

Problem

How do cells, tissues, and organs differ in structure and function?

Pre-Lab Discussion

Read the entire investigation. Then work with a partner to answer the following questions.

1. Part C is titled "Examination of Chicken Organs." What organs will you examine in this part of the investigation?

   _____

2. Which layer of chicken skin is composed of dead cells?

   _____

3. How can you prove that an eggshell is made up of at least two layers?

   _____

4. Why do some muscles appear to run in different directions?

   _____

5. What is the function of the chalazae?

   _____

Materials (per group)

whole chicken, cut up,
     and including the liver,
     heart, and gizzard
chicken egg
dissecting probe or toothpick
scalpel or single-edged razor blade
compound light microscope

microscope slide
coverslip
dissecting probe
dropper pipette
eosin Y solution
plastic gloves

Safety ⛊🧤🔬🔥☠️🔥🔥

Put on a laboratory apron. Be careful when handling sharp instruments. Always handle the microscope with extreme care. If you are using a microscope with a lamp, follow all safety rules related to electrical equipment. You are responsible for its proper care and use. Always use special caution when working with laboratory chemicals, as they may irritate or stain skin or clothing. Never touch or taste any chemical unless instructed to do so. Wear plastic gloves when handling raw chicken or eggs, or tools that have been in contact with them. Wash hands thoroughly after carrying out this investigation. Note all safety alert symbols next to the steps in the Procedure and review the meaning of each symbol by referring to Safety Symbols on page 8.

Procedure

Part A. Examination of a Chicken Egg

 1. Obtain a chicken egg that has been broken into a dish. Also obtain a piece of the eggshell.

2. Notice the tiny bit of white that has floated to the top of the yolk. This is the egg cell, or ovum, itself. The yolk is a food storage packet for the developing chicken. Notice that the yolk is held into a round shape by a thin membrane.

3. Look for two twisted, white strings in the egg white. These strings are called chalazae. The chalazae help to keep the yolk more or less in the center of the white.

4. Another membrane surrounds the egg white. You can probably find remnants of this outer membrane by examining a piece of the eggshell. Although the shell looks as though it consists of one layer, it is actually made up of three layers. One way to prove that there are at least two layers is to examine a brown eggshell. It is brown on the outside but white on the inside. The eggshell also contains pores through which air enters and waste gases escape.

5. On the egg diagram in Figure 1, label the following structures: eggshell, outer membrane, egg white, chalaza, yolk, yolk membrane, ovum.

Part B. Examination of Chicken Tissues

1. Obtain a chicken wing and either a breast, a thigh, or a drumstick. Examine the skin first. Notice that the chicken skin is covered with "goose bumps." Each bump is a pocket from which a feather used to grow. Look along the rear edge of a wing to see if you can find a pin feather. A pin feather is the soft root of a feather that did not come out when the bird was plucked. Label the pin feather and goose bump muscle in the skin diagram in Figure 2.

2. Both your skin and the chicken skin are actually composed of two layers. The epidermis, or outer layer, is composed of dead cells. The thicker, inside layer is called the dermis. Under these two layers, you will notice a layer of fat. Label the following additional structures in Figure 2: epidermis, dermis, fat.

3. Most of the meat we eat, including chicken, is muscle tissue. Examine the muscles of a chicken breast, thigh, or drumstick. Pick at the muscle tissue with a dissecting probe, scalpel, or toothpick and you will see that it is made up of separate muscle fibers.

4. Locate some of the thin, transparent connective tissue that holds one layer of muscle to another. Connective tissue also includes the gristle, or cartilage, at the end of the meat on a chicken leg. This gristle is actually a tendon that connects muscle to bone. Muscles located on either side of a layer of gristle usually run in somewhat different directions. This is because muscles generally work in pairs, pulling in opposite directions. Lable the muscle in Figure 2.

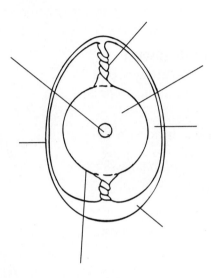

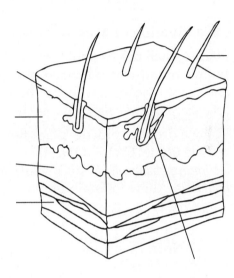

Figure 1

Figure 2

Part C. Examination of Chicken Organs

1. Obtain a chicken liver. Notice its shape, color, and texture. In the spaces below, describe the shape, color, and texture of the chicken liver.

_____

_____

2. Obtain a chicken gizzard that is cut into halves. Examine the cut surface. In the spaces below, describe the chicken gizzard. Is it harder or softer than the liver?

_____

3. Obtain a chicken heart that has been cut in half lengthwise. Notice that the heart is divided into sections called chambers. See if you can locate the large blood vessels that connect to the top chambers. In the space below, describe the chicken heart. How many chambers, or sections, does it have?

_____

4. List the various cells, tissues, and organs you have examined in this investigation.

Cells:

_____

Tissues:

_____

_____

Organs:

_____

_____

Part D. Examination of Muscle Tissue

1. Place a small piece of chicken on the dissecting tray. Remove a sample of muscle tissue from the chicken with the dissecting probe and place it on a microscope slide. **CAUTION:** *The dissecting probe is very sharp. Handle the probe carefully to prevent cuts.*

2. Using a dropper pipette, place two drops of eosin Y solution on the muscle tissue. **CAUTION:** *Always use special caution when handling laboratory chemicals. Eosin Y solution will stain skin and other porous materials.* Allow the stain to remain on the tissue for two minutes.

3. After two minutes, remove the excess stain by dipping the corner of a paper towel into the stain and allowing the towel to draw up the liquid. **Note:** *Do not rub the towel on the sample, as it may disturb or destroy the fibers.*

4. Use a dropper pipette to place two drops of water on the tissue. Wait two minutes and then remove the excess water as you removed the excess stain.

5. Add two drops of water to the tissue and place the coverslip on the microscope slide. Using the handle of a dissecting probe, tap the coverslip gently to flatten the tissue. Tap gently to avoid breaking the coverslip.

6. Use the low-power objective to find a stained muscle cell or group of cells. The cells are long, narrow, and tapered. **CAUTION:** *If your microscope has a lamp, follow all safety procedures related to electrical equipment.*

7. Carefully switch to the high-power objective and adjust your microscope slide so that you are focusing on the cells. **CAUTION:** *When turning to the high-power objective, always look at the objective from the side of the microscope so that the objective does not hit or damage the slide.* Notice the general shape of the fibers, the pattern of dark and light stripes, and the number of nuclei. Draw your observations and record the magnification in the space provided on page 85.

8. Return all materials to your teacher for sterilization or disposal. Be sure to wash your hands thoroughly after completing this investigation.

Magnification _____

Observations of Chicken Muscle Fibers

Analysis and Conclusions

1. **Inferring** Why is it important for an eggshell to contain pores through which air can enter and wastes can escape?

_____

_____

_____

2. **Inferring** Why is it an advantage for a chicken to have a layer of fat beneath its skin?

_____

_____

_____

3. **Drawing Conclusions** The liver is a chemical factory. Harmful chemicals are broken down there and reassembled into harmless ones. The liver also stores pale yellow fat. You may have noticed that some chicken livers are yellower and paler than others. What can you conclude about these lighter-colored livers?

_____

_____

_____

4. **Observing, Inferring** How can you describe the general shape of the muscle fibers you examined? How does this shape relate to muscle movement?

_____

_____

_____

5. **Drawing Conclusions** Attached to each "goose bump" on a chicken's skin is a tiny muscle that holds a feather. When the chicken gets cold, the tiny muscles contract. This pulls the feather upright and allows air to be trapped between the ruffled feathers. The air forms an insulating layer against the cold. Humans have goose bumps also. The muscles attached to human goose bumps hold hairs instead of feathers. When you get cold, your goose bumps become more visible. Why does this happen?

_____

_____

_____

6. **Drawing Conclusions** The most powerful muscle in most birds is the pectoral, or breast, muscle. Why do you think this is so?

_____

_____

_____

Going Further

Cut a very thin slice of liver, heart, or gizzard and examine under a microscope, as you examined the muscle fibers in Part D. How do these cells differ from the muscle fibers? How are they similar?

Name_____ Class_____ Date _____

Investigating the Effect of Light Intensity on Photosynthesis

Introduction

In order to carry out photosynthesis, a plant must have light. But how much light? Some plants need a lot of light. Others seem to thrive in shade. Does more light lead to more photosynthesis? In this investigation, you will examine how the intensity of light affects photosynthesis.

Problem

How does light intensity affect the rate of photosynthesis?

Pre-Lab Discussion

Read the entire investigation. Then, work with a partner to answer the following questions.

1. What are the products of photosynthesis? Which of these products is released from leaves as a gas?

   _____

2. What can you tell about photosynthesis if a leaf begins to produce more gas bubbles? Fewer gas bubbles?

   _____

3. What are the manipulated and responding variables in this experiment? Identify one controlled variable.

   _____

   _____

   _____

   _____

4. Predict how you think the intensity of light will affect photosynthesis.

   _____

   _____

Materials

test tube
400-mL beaker
freshly cut sprig of
      an evergreen (such as yew)
forceps
source of bright light
sodium bicarbonate solution
hand lens

watch or clock with second indicator
plastic gloves

Safety

Wear your safety goggles and laboratory apron at all times during this investigation. Be careful not to break any glassware. Note all safety alert symbols next to the steps in the Procedure and review the meaning of each symbol by referring to Safety Symbols on page 8.

Procedure

1. Working with a partner, completely fill a test tube and a beaker with a sodium bicarbonate solution. Sodium bicarbonate will provide a source of carbon dioxide.

2. Using forceps, place a sprig of evergreen about halfway down in the test tube. Be sure that the cut end of the sprig points downward in the test tube.

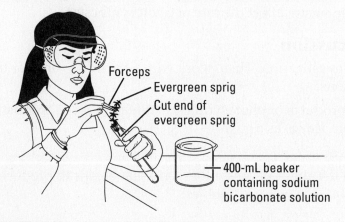

Forceps
Evergreen sprig
Cut end of evergreen sprig
400-mL beaker containing sodium bicarbonate solution

Figure 1

3. Cover the mouth of the test tube with your thumb and turn the test tube upside down. Try not to trap any air bubbles in the test tube.

Test tube containing sodium bicarbonate solution and evergreen sprig

Figure 2

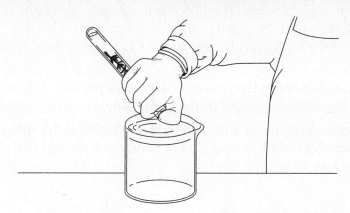

Figure 3

4. Place the mouth of the test tube under the surface of the sodium bicarbonate solution in the beaker. Remove your thumb from the mouth of the test tube.

Figure 4

5. Gently lower the test tube inside the beaker so that the test tube leans against the side of the beaker.

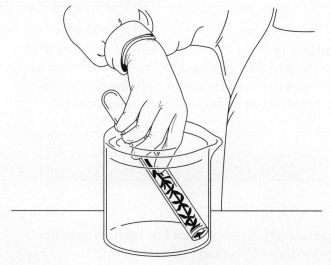

Figure 5

6. Put the beaker in a place where it will receive normal room light. Using a hand lens, count the number of bubbles produced by the sprig in the test tube for 5 minutes. Record the number of bubbles in the Data Table.

7. Darken the room and count the number of bubbles produced again for 5 minutes. Record the number in the Data Table.

8. Turn up the lights in the room and shine a bright light on the sprig. Count the number of bubbles produced in 5 minutes. Record the number in the Data Table.

Data Table

Light Intensity	Number of Bubbles Produced in 5 Minutes
Room light	
Dim light	
Bright light	

Analysis and Conclusions

1. **Observing** From what part of the sprig (stem or needle leaves) did the bubbles emerge?

_____

_____

2. **Observing** When was the greatest number of bubbles produced?

_____

_____

3. **Drawing Conclusions** How does the intensity of light affect the rate of photosynthesis?

_____

_____

4. **Comparing and Contrasting** How do your results compare with those of your classmates? Are they similar? Different? How can you account for any differences in the numbers of bubbles produced? Can you identify any trends even if the actual numbers differ?

_____

_____

_____

Going Further

Perform the activity again using different colors of light. What effect does each color have on the rate of photosynthesis?

Observing Respiration

Introduction

All living things undergo respiration. During this process, food molecules are broken down. As part of this process animals take in oxygen and release carbon dioxide by breathing, which is easily observable. Plants do not "breathe" as animals do, so respiration in plants is not as easily observable. How do we know that plants respire?

In this investigation, you will observe the release of carbon dioxide by humans. You also will perform an experiment to determine whether plants release carbon dioxide as a product of respiration.

Problem

How can the release of carbon dioxide by humans be observed? Do plants release carbon dioxide as a product of respiration?

Pre-Lab Discussion

Read the entire investigation. Then, work with a partner to answer the following questions.

1. What hypothesis is Part A of this experiment testing?

   _____

2. What is an acid indicator?

   _____

3. When the cabbage is mixed with the boiling water, what color do you expect the water to turn?

   _____

4. In Part B, why is nothing added to one of the test tubes containing cabbage indicator?

   _____

5. What special safety note should you observe when you blow through the straw?

   _____

Materials (per group)

distilled water   10 radish seedlings
hot plate   test tubes
2 500-mL beakers   test-tube rack
purple cabbage leaves   stoppers
large slotted spoon   forceps
straw   heat-resistant gloves
cotton ball   plastic gloves

Safety 🐚🏭🧤💧⛏🧯✋

Put on a laboratory apron. Put on safety goggles and plastic gloves. Be careful to avoid breakage when working with glassware. Use extreme care when working with heated equipment or materials to avoid burns. Observe proper laboratory procedures when using electrical appliances. Never taste anything used in this laboratory activity. Note all safety alert symbols in the Procedure and review the meaning of each symbol by referring to Safety Symbols on page 8.

Procedure

🐚🏭🧤 **1.** Tear the purple cabbage into small pieces. Place the cabbage pieces into one of the beakers.

⛏🧯 **2.** Pour about 300 mL of distilled water into the other beaker. Using the hot plate, heat the water until it boils. **CAUTION:** *Put on safety goggles. Be careful when working with the hot plate.*

💧 **3.** Put on heat-resistant gloves. Pour the hot distilled water into the bowl that contains the cabbage. **CAUTION:** *Be careful when working with heated materials to avoid burns.* Allow the water to cool. Remove the heat-resistant gloves. The water will turn purplish-blue in color when mixed with the cabbage.

✋ **4.** Using the slotted spoon, remove the cabbage pieces and discard them according to your teacher's directions. Save the liquid to use as an acid indicator. Its color will change from purplish-blue to reddish-blue when it is mixed with an acid. When carbon dioxide combines with water, it forms a weak acid called carbonic acid.

5. Pour some of the cabbage indicator into 2 test tubes so that each is half full. Cover one test tube completely with aluminum foil.

6. Use a straw to blow a few times into the uncovered test tube, as shown in Figure 1. **CAUTION:** *Be sure not to inhale any of the cabbage indicator.* Observe any changes in the color of the cabbage indicator in both test tubes. Record your observations in the Data Table.

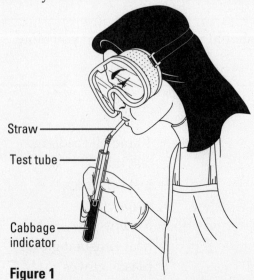

Straw —

Test tube —

Cabbage — indicator

Figure 1

7. Pour some of the cabbage indicator into 2 test tubes so that they are one-quarter full.

8. Place a cotton ball and 10 radish seedlings in one test tube. See Figure 2. Place a stopper in both test tubes. Place the test tubes in a test-tube rack and set them aside for 24 hours.

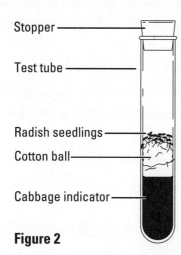

Stopper

Test tube

Radish seedlings

Cotton ball

Cabbage indicator

Figure 2

9. After 24 hours, observe the test tubes. Record your observations in the Data Table.

Data Table

Test Tube	Description	Color of Cabbage Indicator
1		
2		
3		
4		

Analysis and Conclusions

1. **Observing** Did the color of the cabbage indicator change when you exhaled into the test tube? Explain why.

_____

_____

_____

2. **Observing** Did the color of the cabbage indicator change in the test tube that contained the radish seedlings? Explain the reason.

_____

_____

_____

3. **Comparing and Contrasting** Compare the reaction that occurred in the test tube that contained the radish seedlings with the one that occurred in the test tube into which you exhaled. How are they similar?

_____

_____

4. **Inferring** Did respiration occur in this experiment? Explain your answer.

_____

_____

5. **Predicting** How would your results have been affected if you had used more seedlings? Fewer seedlings?

_____

_____

_____

6. **Inferring** Why were seedlings used in this investigation rather than adult plants?

_____

_____

_____

7. **Drawing Conclusions** Why is the process of cellular respiration common to all forms of life?

_____

_____

8. **Inferring** Why do most living things take in oxygen?

_____

_____

Going Further

Why do we need plants? Why do plants need animals? What might happen if too many trees are destroyed? Use what you know about photosynthesis and respiration to answer these questions.

Chapter 10   Cell Growth and Division

Observing Specialized Cells

Introduction

The cell is the basic unit of structure and function in all living things. All of the processes necessary for life occur in cells. In single-celled organisms, such as amoebas, all of the functions required by the organism take place within one cell. Multicellular organisms, such as humans and plants, are made up of many cells with different structures and functions. The shape and size of a cell, as well as the structures found inside it, are determined by the functions of the cell. In this investigation, you will observe several different types of cells. You will compare and contrast the structures you see in the cells, and relate the structures to the functions the different cells perform.

Problem

How are the structures of specialized cells adapted to fit their particular functions?

Pre-Lab Discussion

Read the entire investigation. Then, work with a partner to answer the following questions.

1. What types of cells have a cell membrane, cytoplasm, and a nucleus? Where would you expect to find the cytoplasm in a cell?

   _____

   _____

2. In what types of cells would you expect to see a cell wall?

   _____

3. Saclike structures called vacuoles are found in many cells. What is the function of vacuoles?

   _____

4. An organelle is a cell structure with a specialized function. Plastids are plant organelles. Which plastid traps the energy of sunlight and converts it into chemical energy?

   _____

5. The outer layer of cells of a leaf is called the epidermis. These cells protect the tissues inside the leaf by slowing down the loss of water through evaporation. Predict what these cells will look like.

   _____

6. Some functions are exclusive to plants, while others are performed only by animals. Which specialized cells or tissues would you expect to find only in plants? Only in animals?

   _____

   _____

Materials *(per group)*

compound light microscope
lens paper
lettuce leaf
water plant leaf
dropper pipette
2 microscope slides
2 coverslips
forceps
dissecting probe
prepared slides of 3 types of human tissues

Safety

Put on a laboratory apron. Handle all glassware and sharp tools carefully. Always handle the microscope with extreme care. If you are using a microscope with a lamp, follow all safety rules related to electrical equipment. You are responsible for its proper care and use. Use caution when handling microscope slides, as they can break easily and cut you. Note all safety alert symbols and review the meaning of each symbol by referring to Safety Symbols on page 8.

Procedure

1. Obtain a microscope and place it about 10 centimeters from the edge of the laboratory table.

2. Carefully clean the eyepiece and the objective lenses with lens paper.

3. Locate a rib in the lettuce leaf. As shown in Figure 1, bend the lettuce leaf against the curve until it snaps.

A

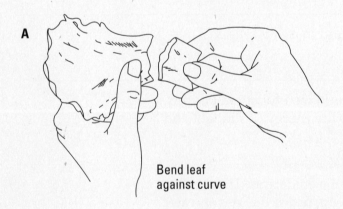

Bend leaf
against curve

B

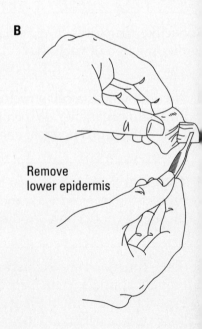

Remove
lower epidermis

Figure 1

4. With the forceps, carefully remove the thin layer of tissue called the epidermis from the piece of lettuce. Spread out the epidermis as smoothly as possible on a microscope slide. **Note:** *If the epidermis becomes folded on the slide, use a dissecting probe to gently unfold and flatten it.* **CAUTION:** *Microscope slides can break easily.*

5. To prepare a wet-mount slide, place a drop of water in the center of the slide. Using the dissecting probe, gently lower the coverslip onto the lettuce as shown in Figure 2. **CAUTION:** *Be careful when handling sharp instruments.*

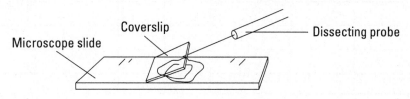

Figure 2

6. Observe the lettuce epidermis under the low-power objective of the microscope. **Note:** *It may be necessary to adjust the diaphragm so there is sufficient light passing through the cells.* Notice the irregular shapes of the epidermal cells.

7. Switch to the high-power objective. **CAUTION:** *When turning to the high-power objective, you should always look at the objective from the side of your microscope so that the objective lens does not hit or damage the slide.*

8. In the Data Table on page 98, write the name of the cell that you examined. Describe its general shape and place a check mark in the columns below the structures that you are able to observe under the high-power objective.

9. In the appropriate place on page 98, draw and label what you see under the high-power objective. Record the magnification of the microscope.

10. Repeat steps 5 to 9 using the water plant leaf.

11. Repeat steps 6 to 9 using the 3 prepared slides of human cells and/or tissues. Draw and label what you see in the appropriate place on pages 98 and 99.

Data Table

Cell Type	Shape	Cell Structures						
		Cell wall	Cell membrane	Nucleus	Nuclear envelope	Cytoplasm	Vacuoles	Plastids

Magnification _____

Lettuce epidermis

Magnification _____

Water plant epidermis

Prepared Slide 1

Magnification _____

Tissue _____

Prepared Slide 2

Magnification _____

Tissue _____

Prepared Slide 3

Magnification _____

Tissue _____

Analysis and Conclusions

1. **Observing** Do all the cells share any common structures? Explain your answer.

_____

_____

_____

2. **Comparing and Contrasting** Compare the shapes of the different cells. Describe any similarities or differences.

_____

_____

_____

3. **Inferring** What factors might affect the size and shape of a cell?

_____

_____

_____

4. **Comparing and Contrasting** For each type of tissue that you observed, describe one feature that is not found in any of the others.

_____

_____

_____

_____

5. **Analyzing Data** How is each tissue you observed adapted to perform its special function?

_____

_____

_____

6. Drawing Conclusions Why do the cells that make up the different tissues have different shapes and sizes?

_____

_____

_____

Going Further

Obtain additional prepared slides of specialized cells and tissue from your teacher. Prepare labeled sketches of each of these slides.

Solving Heredity Problems

Introduction

Inheritable characteristics of organisms are passed from parents to offspring by genes. Four terms are used to describe organisms genetically. Genotype describes an organism's genetic makeup. Genotypes made up of like alleles are homozygous; those made up of unlike alleles are heterozygous. Phenotype describes an organism's appearance and is based on the organism's genotype.

In this investigation, you will solve two different heredity problems. The first problem is concerned with the color of hair in guinea pigs. The second problem is concerned with codominance.

Problem

What are the possible genotypes and phenotypes of offspring produced by parent organisms with known characteristics?

Pre-Lab Discussion

Read the entire investigation. Then, work with a partner to answer the following questions.

1. In pea plants, the allele for purple flower color is dominant. The allele for white flower color is recessive. Write the genotype of a pea plant that is heterozygous for flower color. What two genotypes might a pea plant homozygous for flower color have?

   _____

   _____

   _____

   _____

   _____

2. Predict the phenotype of a pea plant with the genotype Pp for flower color. (Hint: Flower color in pea plants is completely dominant.)

   _____

3. What is the difference between alleles that are codominant and those that are completely dominant?

   _____

   _____

   _____

   _____

   _____

4. What do the boxes in a Punnett square represent? How will you use the boxes to calculate genotypic ratios?

_____

_____

_____

_____

_____

_____

5. For a given Punnett square, will the genotypic ratio always be the same as the phenotypic ratio? Explain your answer.

_____

_____

_____

_____

_____

Procedure

1. In guinea pigs, the allele for black fur (*B*) is dominant over the allele for white fur (*b*). Fill in the Punnett square in Figure 1 to determine the possible genotypes and phenotypes of offspring produced from the cross between a homozygous black guinea pig and a heterozygous black guinea pig.

Phenotype: black
Genotype: homozygous

	B	B
B	Genotype: _____ Phenotype: _____	Genotype: _____ Phenotype: _____
b	Genotype: _____ Phenotype: _____	Genotype: _____ Phenotype: _____

Phenotype: black
Genotype: heterozygous

Figure 1

2. In cattle, codominance of the allele for a red coat (*R*) and the allele for a white coat (*W*) results in offspring with a roan coat (*RW*); that is, a coat with both red and white hairs. Fill in the Punnett square in Figure 2 to determine the possible genotypes and phenotypes of offspring produced from the cross between a roan cow and a white bull.

Phenotype: _____

	R	W
W	Genotype: _____ Phenotype: _____	Genotype: _____ Phenotype: _____
W	Genotype: _____ Phenotype: _____	Genotype: _____ Phenotype: _____

Phenotype: _____

Figure 2

Analysis and Conclusions

1. **Calculating** What is the genotypic ratio in Figure 1?

_____

2. **Calculating** What is the phenotypic ratio in Figure 1?

_____

3. **Drawing Conclusions** Is it possible to produce a white guinea pig by crossing a homozygous black guinea pig and a heterozygous black guinea pig? Explain your answer.

_____

_____

_____

_____

4. **Calculating** What is the genotypic ratio in Figure 2?

_____

5. **Calculating** What is the phenotypic ratio in Figure 2?

_____

6. **Using Tables** What would the genotypes and phenotypes of the offspring be from the cross between a roan cow and a roan bull? Draw a Punnett square below to support your answer.

_____

_____

_____

7. Is it possible for two organisms to have different genotypes but the same phenotype? Explain your answer.

_____

_____

_____

_____

Going Further

Animal and plant breeders often keep careful records about the phenotypes of the organisms they raise—often in the form of a pedigree. Find examples of pedigrees and trace the inheritance of traits from one generation to the next. Why do you think pedigrees and careful records might be important to breeders?

Investigating Gel Electrophoresis

Introduction

Agarose gel electrophoresis is a commonly used method of separating molecules based on their charge, size, and shape. It is especially useful in separating charged molecules of DNA and RNA. When an electric current is applied to the gel, negatively charged molecules move toward the positive electrode (anode), and positively charged molecules move toward the negative electrode (cathode). The charge, size, and shape of a particular molecule all affect the rate at which a molecule moves through the gel.

In this investigation, you will compare the rate and direction of movement of several different dye samples in an agarose gel and draw conclusions about their charge and chemical composition based on your observations.

Problem

How can gel electrophoresis be used to separate different molecules?

Pre-Lab Discussion

Read the entire investigation. Then, work with a partner to answer the following questions.

1. Why should you use a clean transfer pipette for each sample?

_____

_____

2. How does gel electrophoresis separate molecules?

_____

_____

3. In which direction do negatively charged molecules move? Positively charged molecules?

_____

_____

4. How will you know if the current is flowing properly in your electrophoresis apparatus?

_____

_____

5. Before you begin the investigation, your gel is transparent. What will it look like at the end of the investigation?

_____

_____

Materials *(per group)*

gel electrophoresis apparatus
direct current power source
transfer pipettes

numbered dye samples
plastic gloves

Safety 🔲🔲🔲🔲🔲🔲🔲

Put on a laboratory apron. Put on safety goggles and plastic gloves. Never taste anything used in this laboratory investigation. Always work with special caution when working with laboratory chemicals, as they may irritate the skin or stain skin or clothing. Observe proper laboratory procedures when using electrical equipment. Use extreme care when working with heated equipment or materials to avoid burns. Wash your hands thoroughly after carrying out this investigation. Note all safety alert symbols in the Procedure and review the meaning of each symbol by referring to Safety Symbols on page 8.

Procedure

1. **CAUTION:** *Put on a laboratory apron, safety goggles, and disposable gloves before beginning this investigation. Do not smell or taste any chemicals in this investigation. If a chemical gets on your clothes or skin, flush the area with water immediately and notify your teacher. When loading the samples into the wells, always point your pipette away from yourself and others, especially the face and eyes.* Using a transfer pipette, carefully load each of the dye samples into the wells in the middle of the gel in consecutive order. Follow your teacher's directions for the proper way to load the samples into the wells. Use a clean transfer pipette for each sample. Load each well until it is full.

2. After loading the samples, carefully close the cover of the apparatus onto the electrode terminals. Be sure to align the negative and positive marks on the cover with the corresponding marks on the apparatus chamber.

3. Insert the plug of the negative (black) wire into the negative (black) input of the power source. Insert the plug of the positive (red) wire into the positive (red) input of the power source. See Figure 1.
   CAUTION: *Do not use electrical equipment near water or with wet hands.*

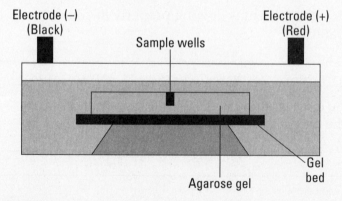

Figure 1

4. Set the power source at the voltage determined by your teacher.

5. Run the electrophoresis for the appropriate length of time based on the voltage you are using as determined by your teacher. Look for bubbles forming on the electrodes to be sure that current is flowing properly.

6. When the electrophoresis is completed, turn off the power, unplug the power source, disconnect the wires, and remove the cover from the apparatus.

7. Carefully remove the gel on its bed, holding each end of the gel to prevent it from slipping off the bed.

8. In Figure 2, indicate the relative positions of the bands of dye.

9. Dispose of all gels, solutions, and equipment according to your teacher's instructions. Wash your hands thoroughly after completing this investigation.

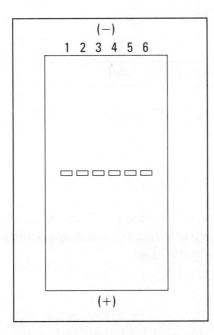

Figure 2: Results of electrophoresis

Analysis and Conclusions

1. **Inferring** Based on your results, which samples have a negative charge? A positive charge?

_____

_____

2. **Drawing Conclusions** What can you conclude about the samples in lanes 4 and 6?

_____

_____

_____

3. **Controlling Variables** What steps did you take during the procedure to avoid contaminating samples?

_____

_____

4. **Inferring** Why might it be important to avoid contaminating DNA samples when doing a DNA analysis?

_____

_____

_____

_____

_____

5. **Analyzing Data** Assume that samples 4 and 6 are each a combination of samples 1–3 or 5. Based on this assumption, can you identify the dyes in samples 4 and 6?

_____

_____

_____

_____

Going Further

In DNA sequencing, strands of DNA are selectively broken into smaller pieces that can then be separated by gel electrophoresis. Using reference materials available in your school or public library or on the Internet, research the process of DNA sequencing. What chemicals are used to break DNA strands into pieces? What are some applications of this process? Present your findings to the class.

Investigating Inherited Traits

Introduction

Heredity is the passing on of traits, or characteristics, from parent to offspring. The genetic makeup of an individual is known as its genotype. The physical traits you can observe in a person are his or her phenotype. Phenotype is a result of the genotype and the individual's interaction with the environment.

The units of heredity are called genes. Genes are found on the chromosomes in a cell. An allele is one of two or more forms of a gene. When the two alleles of a pair are the same, the genotype is homozygous, or pure. When the two alleles are not the same, the genotype is heterozygous, or hybrid. In nature, specific combinations of alleles happen only by chance.

Some alleles are expressed only when the dominant allele is absent. These alleles produce recessive phenotypes. Alleles that are expressed when the genotype is either homozygous or heterozygous produce dominant phenotypes. An allele that codes for a dominant trait is represented by a capital letter, while an allele that codes for a recessive trait is represented by a lowercase letter.

Sometimes when the genotype is heterozygous, neither the dominant nor recessive phenotype occurs. In this case, called incomplete dominance or codominance, an intermediate phenotype is produced.

In humans, the sex of a person is determined by the combination of two sex chromosomes. People who have two X chromosomes (XX) are females, while those who have one X chromosome and one Y chromosome (XY) are males.

In this investigation, you will see how different combinations of alleles produce different characteristics.

Problem

How are traits inherited?

Pre-Lab Discussion

Read the entire investigation. Then, work with a partner to answer the following questions.

1. What does a single side of the coin or disk represent?

_____

_____

2. What are the chances that any coin or disk tossed will land heads up?

_____

_____

3. How is a coin toss like the selection of a particular allele?

_____

_____

4. For the traits in this investigation, do all heterozygous pairs of alleles produce an intermediate phenotype?

_____

_____

5. Can you accurately determine a person's genotype by observing his or her phenotype?

_____

_____

Materials _(per pair)_

3 textbooks
2 coins

Procedure

1. Place the textbooks on the laboratory table so that they form a triangular well.

2. Obtain two coins. You and your partner will each flip a coin to determine the traits in a hypothetical offspring.

3. Start by determining the sex of the offspring. Flip the coins into the well. If both coins land the same side up, the offspring is a female. If the coins land different sides up, the offspring is a male. Record the sex of the offspring in the blank on page 117.

4. For the rest of the coin tosses you will make, heads will represent the dominant allele and tails will represent the recessive allele.

5. You and your partner should now flip your coins into the well at the same time to determine the phenotype of the first trait, the shape of the face. **Note:** _The coins should be flipped only once for each trait._ After each flip, record the trait of your offspring by placing a check in the appropriate box in Figure 1.

6. Continue to flip the coins for each trait listed in the table in Figure 1. **Note:** _Some information in Figure 1 has been simplified. Some listed traits are actually produced by two or more genes._

7. Using the recorded traits, draw the facial features for your offspring in the space provided on page 117.

Name_______________________________ Class__________________ Date ______________

Traits	Dominant (both heads)	Hybrid (one head, one tail)	Recessive (both tails)
Shape of face	round *RR*	round *Rr*	Square *rr*
Cleft in chin	present *CC*	present *Cc*	absent *cc*
Texture of hair	curly *HH*	wavy *Hh*	straight *hh*
Widow's peak	present *WW*	present *Ww*	absent *ww*
Spacing of eyes	close together *EE*	medium distance *Ee*	far apart *ee*
Shape of eyes	almond *AA*	almond *Aa*	round *aa*
Position of eyes	straight *SS*	straight *Ss*	slant upward *ss*
Size of eyes	large *LL*	medium *Ll*	small *ll*

Figure 1

Traits	Dominant (both heads)	Hybrid (one head, one tail)	Recessive (both tails)
Length of eyelashes	long *LL*	long *Ll*	short *ll*
Shape of eyebrows	bushy *BB*	bushy *Bb*	fine *bb*
Position of eyebrows	not connected *NN*	not connected *Nn*	connected *nn*
Size of nose	large *LL*	medium *Ll*	small *ll*
Shape of lips	thick *TT*	medium *Tt*	thin *tt*
Size of ears	large *LL*	medium *Ll*	small *ll*
Size of mouth	large *LL*	medium *Ll*	small *ll*
Freckles	present *FF*	present *Ff*	absent *ff*
Dimples	present *DD*	present *Dd*	absent *dd*

Figure 1 *continued*

Name_____ Class_____ Date _____

Sex of offspring

_____

Drawing of Offspring

Analysis and Conclusions

1. **Calculating** What percent chance did you and your partner have of "producing" a male offspring? A female offspring? Explain your answer.

_____

_____

_____

2. **Predicting** Would you expect the other pairs of students in your class to have an offspring completely similar to yours? Explain your answer.

_____

_____

_____

3. **Inferring** What are the possible genotypes of the parents of a child who has wavy hair *(Hh)*?

_____

_____

4. **Classifying** Which traits in this investigation showed incomplete dominance?

_____

_____

5. **Drawing Conclusions** Do you think that anyone in your class has all the same genetic traits that you have? Explain your answer.

_____

_____

_____

6. **Drawing Conclusions** How might it be possible for you to show a trait when none of your relatives shows it?

_____

_____

_____

Going Further

Repeat this investigation with your partner to "produce" your second offspring. After completing all of your tosses, make a drawing of the offspring. What similarities exist between your first and second offspring? What differences? Would you expect a third offspring to resemble either the first or the second offspring? Explain your reason.

Modeling Camouflage and Natural Selection

Introduction

As part of his theory of evolution by natural selection, Charles Darwin proposed that organisms best adapted to their environment survive and reproduce more successfully than other organisms. Camouflage, the concealment of an organism because of its color, is an example of an adaptation that can increase an organism's chance of surviving to reproduce. Organisms that are more difficult for predators to see are less likely to be attacked. In this investigation, you will examine the effect of camouflage on the survival of a prey species.

Problem

How does camouflage affect natural selection in a prey species?

Pre-Lab Discussion

Read the entire investigation. Then, work with a partner to answer the following questions.

1. What in nature does the floral-patterned background represent?

_____

_____

_____

2. Do you expect the predator to pick up an equal number of dots of each color? Explain why you think that.

_____

_____

3. Which of the colored dots do you expect to best "survive" attack by the predator?

_____

4. Would an organism that is camouflaged in its usual environment be camouflaged in all environments? Explain your answer.

_____

_____

_____

5. How might the results of this experiment change if the same dots were scattered on a multicolored background of colors that differs from the one that you use?

_____

_____

_____

Materials *(per group)*

hole punch
colored construction paper (1 sheet of each
 of the following colors: black, blue, brown,
 green, orange, purple, red, white, yellow)
9 sealable plastic bags
80 cm × 80 cm piece of floral paper or cloth
transparent tape

Safety

Be careful when handling sharp instruments. Note the safety alert
symbol next to step 1 in the Procedure and review the meaning of the
symbol by referring to Safety Symbols on page 8.

Procedure

1. Punch 10 dots of each color from the sheets of colored construction
 paper. Put the dots for each color in a different plastic bag.
 CAUTION: *Be careful not to pinch or cut your fingers with the hole punch.*

2. Spread a piece of floral paper or cloth on a flat surface. Use
 transparent tape to attach each corner of the paper or cloth to the
 flat surface.

3. Choose one member of your group to be the recorder and another
 to be the predator. The other members of the group will be the prey.

4. Have the predator look away while the prey randomly spread the
 dots of each color over the paper.

5. Have the predator turn back to the paper and immediately pick up
 the first dot he or she sees, and then put that dot aside.

6. In the Data Table, have the recorder make a tally mark in the correct
 row in the center column. Then across from that, in the column on
 the right, the recorder should write in the color of the background
 where the dot was found.

7. Repeat steps 5 and 6 until a total of 10 dots have been picked up.
 Make sure that the predator looks away before a selection is made
 each time.

8. In the center column of the Data Table, have the recorder write the
 total number of dots selected by the predator.

9. Have the recorder and the predator reverse roles. While the
 predator looks away, return the 10 selected dots to the multicolored
 surface. Then repeat steps 5 through 8.

10. Have one student from your group record your group data in a
 class data table drawn on the chalkboard.

Name_____ Class_____ Date _____

Data Table

Color of Dot	Total Number of Dots Recovered	Background Colors (List)
Black		
Blue		
Brown		
Green		
Orange		
Purple		
Red		
White		
Yellow		

Analysis and Conclusions

1. **Comparing and Contrasting** Which color dot was picked up most frequently? Which color dot was picked up least frequently?

   _____

   _____

   _____

   _____

2. **Analyzing Data** How did the dots picked up most frequently differ from those that were picked up least frequently?

   _____

   _____

   _____

3. **Comparing and Contrasting** How did your group's results compare with the results of other groups?

   _____

   _____

   _____

4. **Drawing Conclusions** If the colored dots represent a species that is preyed upon, what does this experiment demonstrate?

   _____

   _____

   _____

5. Predicting Based on this model, if the original mixture of dots represents varied colors in the members of a population, what would likely happen to that population over many generations?

_____

_____

_____

_____

Going Further

The appearance of some animals changes as their environment changes. Using library materials or the Internet, research animals such as the snowshoe hare, arctic hare, arctic fox, and the gray wolf. Write a short paragraph describing seasonal changes in the appearance of these animals, and how these changes may help the animal survive.

Modeling Natural Selection

Introduction

In the process of natural selection, organisms that are better adapted to their environment than other members of their species reproduce more successfully. This difference in reproduction causes evolution— that is, a gradual change in the genes of a population. In this investigation, you will examine how natural selection results in evolution in a small population of animals.

Problem

How does natural selection bring about a change in the genetic makeup of a population?

Pre-Lab Discussion

Read the entire investigation. Then, work with a partner to answer the following questions.

1. What advantage does a white mouse have over a brown one in a white sand dune environment?

_____

_____

2. In this experiment, is chance a factor in determining whether or not a brown mouse survives? Explain your answer.

_____

_____

_____

3. Do you expect the proportion of brown mice to white mice to increase from one generation to the next? Explain your answer.

_____

_____

_____

4. In this experimental model, two variables interact to influence the responding variable. What are these two independent variables?

_____

_____

5. What is the responding variable?

_____

Materials *(per group)*

scissors   white crayon or chalk
metric ruler   marking pen
black construction paper   25 index cards

Safety

Be careful when handling sharp instruments. Note the safety alert symbol next to step 1 in the Procedure and review the meaning of the symbol by referring to Safety Symbols on page 8.

Procedure

Part A. Building the Model

1. Cut out 50 6-cm-square cards from the black construction paper. **CAUTION:** *Be careful when handling the scissors. Point the blades away from you when you cut.*

2. Using the white crayon or chalk, mark 25 of the black cards on one side with a capital "W." These cards will represent the allele that codes for white fur, which is dominant.

3. Mark the other 25 black cards on one side with a lowercase "w." These cards will represent the the allele that codes for brown fur, which is recessive.

4. Mark 15 of the index cards on one side with an "X." These cards will represent predators. Leave the rest of the index cards blank.

5. Shuffle the black cards so that the W cards and the w cards are mixed together at random. Then place the stack of black cards face down on a desk or table.

6. Shuffle the index cards so that the predator cards and the blank cards are mixed together. Then place the stack of index cards face down next to the black cards.

Part B. Using the Model

1. Draw the two top cards from the stack of black cards. If the two cards together read WW or Ww, you have a white mouse. If they read ww, you have a brown mouse. Record the type of mouse you have by making a tally mark in the appropriate column next to Generation 1 in the Data Table.

Data Table

Generation	White Mice	Brown Mice	Live	Die
1				
2				
3				
4				

2. Use the model to study the survival of white mice and brown mice in a white sandy desert. Draw the top card from the stack of index cards. If you choose a card with an X and you have a brown mouse, the mouse will be caught and eaten by the predator. If you choose a card with an X and you have a white mouse, the mouse will escape the predator by hiding in the white sand and live. If you choose a blank card, there is no predator and either color mouse will live.

3. Record the fate of your mouse by making a tally mark in the appropriate column of the Data Table. If your mouse survived, return the black cards to the bottom of the stack. If your mouse died, set aside the black cards. Then return the index card to the bottom of the stack.

4. Repeat steps 1–3 until you have selected all 25 pairs of cards. This completes the first generation of mice.

5. Count the number of black cards still remaining in the stack. On the line below, record the number of allele pairs remaining. (This is the total number of black cards divided by 2.)

_____

6. Repeat steps 1–3 as many times as you have allele pairs remaining. Record your results in the Data Table next to Generation 2.

7. Count the number of black cards remaining in the stack. On the line below, record the number of allele pairs remaining.

_____

8. Repeat step 6, but this time record your results next to Generation 3 in the Data Table.

9. Count the number of black cards. On the line below, record the number of allele pairs remaining.

_____

10. Repeat step 6, but this time record your results next to Generation 4 in the Data Table.

Analysis and Conclusions

1. **Analyzing Data** How many brown mice were produced in the first generation?

_____

2. **Comparing and Contrasting** How did the proportion of brown mice produced in the third and fourth generations compare to the proportion produced in the first generation?

_____

_____

3. **Evaluating** Which allele, *W* or *w*, was removed from the gene pool by predation?

_____

4. Using Models Does this model illustrate the concept of evolution by natural selection? Explain your answer.

_____

_____

_____

5. Predicting If the main predator of mice in this white-sand desert were an animal that hunted by smell rather than sight, would you expect the same results as this model produced? Explain your reason.

_____

_____

_____

Going Further

In this experimental model, the total number of mice decreases each generation. Do you think this represents what would occur in a real situation? In a brief paragraph, explain how you could change the model to make it more realistic.

Modeling Index Fossils

Introduction

A fossil is the remains or evidence of an ancient living thing. Fossils of organisms that lived on Earth for only a short time are called index fossils. In this activity you will discover how index fossils can be used to determine the relative ages of rock formations.

Problem

How can index fossils help determine the relative ages of rock formations?

Pre-Lab Discussion

Read the entire investigation. Then work with a partner to answer the following questions.

1. What do the sand and the salt in the beakers represent?

_____

2. How will you determine the number of "Years Ago" that leaves appeared?

_____

_____

3. Which line in the Data Table represents the present time?

_____

4. In the Data Table, how many millions of years are represented by 1 minute?

_____

5. What is an index fossil?

_____

Materials *(per group)*

scissors	small leaves
construction paper	watch or clock with second hand
3 500-mL beakers or glass jars	sand
glass-marking pencil	table salt

Safety 🖐🧥🧤🔪🗑🧪

Put on safety goggles. Put on a laboratory apron. Be careful to avoid breakage when working with glassware. Use caution with sharp instruments. Wash your hands thoroughly after handling plant materials and after carrying out this investigation. Note all safety alert symbols next to the steps in the Procedure and review the meaning of each symbol by referring to Safety Symbols on page 8.

Procedure

1. Cut a large circle from a piece of construction paper. The circle represents Earth.

2. Use a glass-marking pencil to label the three beakers A, B, and C.

3. Place the construction-paper circle on a desk or table. Place each beaker in a different location on the circle. Each beaker represents the site of a rock formation on Earth.

4. Place a pile of small leaves near, but not on, the circle. The leaves represent an organism that once lived on Earth.

5. Choose a starting time a few minutes from now, and write that time in column 1 of the Data Table opposite the word "start." Then list the times at 3-minute intervals for the next 30 minutes. Your last time should be written opposite the word "stop."

6. In this activity 30 minutes represent 30 million years in Earth's history. In the column labeled "Years Ago (millions)," list the number of years represented by the times in column 1. Begin by writing "30" in the "start" row, then subtract 3 for each of the next 3-minute periods. You should end up with 0 in the "stop" row.

7. With one partner serving as timer, wait until your watch or clock shows the starting time. Then, add about 2 cm of sand to beaker C. The sand represents a layer in the rock formation.

8. At the next listed time, add a 2-cm layer of table salt to beaker C. The salt represents another layer in the rock formation.

9. At the next listed time, add a layer of sand to both beakers A and C.

10. At the next listed time, add a layer of salt to beakers A and C.

11. At the next listed time, add a layer of sand to beakers A and C.

12. The next time listed in the Data Table should correspond with the event "leaves appear." Move the pile of leaves onto the circle. At the correct time, add a layer of salt to beakers A, B, and C. As you add the salt, also add a leaf to each beaker so that the leaf becomes embedded in the salt. Be sure that you can see each leaf clearly throught the side of its beaker.

13. At the next listed time, move the leaves that you have not used off the circle and back onto the table. (This should correspond with the event "leaves die out" in the Data Table.) After you remove the leaves, add a layer of sand to beakers A and B.

14. At the next listed time, add a layer of salt to beakers A and B.

15. At the next listed time, add a layer of sand to beaker B.

16. At the next listed time, add a layer of salt to beaker B.

17. By now you should have reached the last time listed in the Data Table. Add a layer of sand to beaker B. Your beakers should now look like those shown in Figure 1.

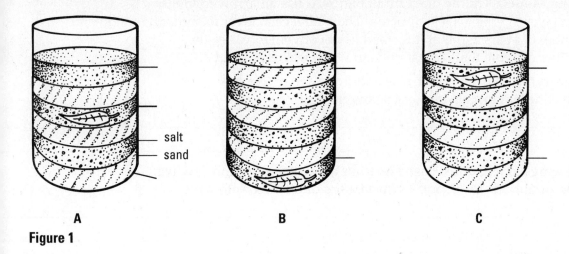

A   B   C

Figure 1

Data Table

Time	Event	Years Ago (millions)
	start	
	leaves appear	
	leaves die out	
	stop	

Analysis and Conclusions

1. **Inferring** In your model, which "rock layers" are older—those on the top or those on the bottom? Explain why.

_____

2. **Calculating** According to your Data Table, how many millions of years ago did leaves appear on Earth? How many millions of years ago did they die out, or become extinct?

_____

3. **Analyzing Data** What must be true about the age of rock layers in which leaves appear? Why do you think so?

_____

_____

4. **Using Models** On the diagram in Figure 1, use an arrow to identify each layer in which a leaf appears. Then label each layer to show the number of years ago that it formed. (For convenience, use the number of years that corresponds to when leaves appeared.)

5. **Classifying** What must be true about the age of the rock layers above the leaf in each beaker? Below the leaf?

_____

_____

6. **Drawing Conclusions** Based on your answer to question 5, which rock formation—A, B, or C—must be the oldest? Explain why.

_____

_____

7. **Inferring** Which rock formation must be the youngest? Why do you think so?

_____

_____

8. **Calculating** Using the leaf as a guide, determine the age of the oldest and youngest rock layer in each beaker. Then label the layers in Figure 1 with this information. Which layers are the oldest and youngest in each beaker?

_____

_____

_____

9. **Drawing Conclusions** How are index fossils used to determine the relative ages of rock formations?

_____

_____

_____

_____

Going Further

Use the library or the Internet to research dinosaurs, and how scientists have determined when they lived. Did all species of dinosaurs live at the same time? Would dinosaur fossils be of any use as index fossils? Explain your answer.

Identifying Vertebrates Using Classification Keys

Introduction

Organisms such as vertebrates (animals with backbones) are classified into groups according to certain characteristics. Using these characteristics, classification keys can be developed. Biologists develop these classification keys so they can be used to identify unfamiliar organisms. Such keys are also useful in studying common characteristics and relationships among organisms.

In this investigation, you will learn to use a simple classification key to identify some organisms.

Problem

How is a classification key used to identify various animals?

Pre-Lab Discussion

Read the entire investigation. Then, work with a partner to answer the following questions.

1. Into which five basic groups will you be classifying vertebrates?

_____

_____

2. What information do you need in order to classify the animals shown in Figure 1? Where will you find this information?

_____

_____

_____

_____

3. What is a classification key?

_____

_____

4. What do the **a** and **b** statements in the classification key describe?

_____

_____

5. Read statement **1b** in the Classification Key for the Extinct Animals shown in Figure 1. If an animal is ectothermic, what is the next step in the key? Explain.

_____

_____

_____

Procedure

1. Vertebrates can be divided into five major groups: fishes, amphibians, reptiles, birds, and mammals. (These are not all formal taxonomic groups.) Fishes have gills. The other vertebrates mentioned have lungs. Fishes, amphibians, and reptiles are called ectothermic because they derive body heat mainly from their environment. (*Ecto-* means outside; *-therm* means heat.) Birds and mammals are called endothermic because they derive body heat mainly from metabolism. (*Endo-* means inside.) Some species in each vertebrate group have become extinct. Ten extinct animals are pictured in Figure 1 on pages 132–134. Study the characteristics of these animals by completing the Data Table on page 134.

Fish (North America)

Pigeon

Bison

Figure 1

Dodo

Elk

Wolf

Tortoise

Figure 1 *continued*

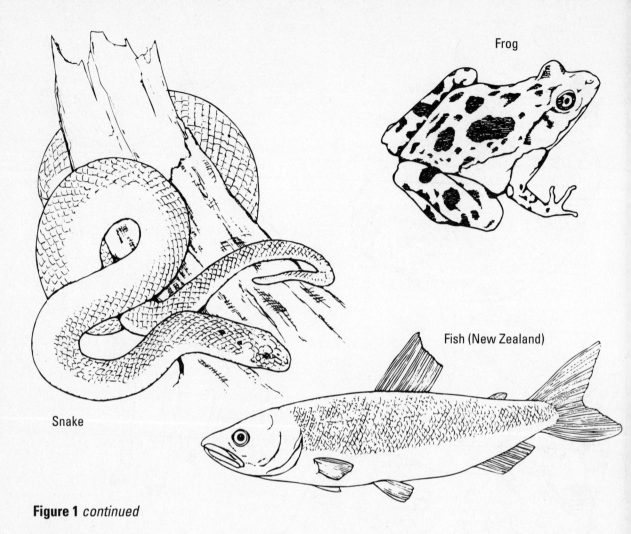

Frog

Snake

Fish (New Zealand)

Figure 1 *continued*

Data Table

Name of Animal	Appendages					Body Covering				Temperature Regulation		Breathing Mechanism	
	Fins	Wings, 2 Legs	Forelegs	Hindlegs	Horns	Smooth skin	Scales	Feathers	Hair/Fur	Ectothermic	Endothermic	Gills	Lungs
Tortoise													
Dodo													
Fish (North America)													
Wolf													
Pigeon													
Elk													
Snake													
Frog													
Bison													
Fish (New Zealand)													

2. The following key is based on information from Figure 1 and the Data Table. Examine how a key works by using it to identify each animal.

Classification Key for the Extinct Animals Shown in Figure 1

1	**a**	Is endothermic	Go to 2
	b	Is ectothermic	Go to 6
2	**a**	Has feathers	Go to 3
	b	Has hair or fur	Go to 4
3	**a**	Has narrow, straight beak	Passenger pigeon
	b	Has wide, crooked beak	Dodo
4	**a**	Has horns	Go to 5
	b	Has no horns	Texas red wolf
5	**a**	Horns may have many branches	Eastern elk
	b	Horns have no branches	Oregon bison
6	**a**	Breathes with gills	Go to 7
	b	Breathes with lungs	Go to 8
7	**a**	Has large, fan-shaped fins just behind the head	Utah Lake sculpin
	b	Has small pectoral fins	New Zealand grayling
8	**a**	Has scaly skin	Go to 9
	b	Has smooth skin	Palestinian painted frog
9	**a**	Has front and hind legs	Domed tortoise
	b	Has no legs	Round Island boa

Analysis and Conclusions

1. **Classifying** Reptiles are ectothermic, have scaly skin, and breathe with lungs. Which of the animals in Figure 1 are reptiles?

_____

2. **Classifying** The Palestinian painted frog is an amphibian. What is one difference between amphibians and reptiles?

_____

3. **Classifying** Mammals are endothermic, have hair or fur, breathe with lungs. (They also give birth to live young.) Which of the animals in Figure 1 are mammals?

_____

4. **Classifying** Birds are endothermic vertebrates with feathers and wings. Which animals in Figure 1 are birds?

_____

5. Drawing Conclusions To which vertebrate group do you belong? Explain.

_____

_____

6. Classifying Develop a classification key for the following mythical creatures. The key has been started for you.

SPHINX:	body of lion, upper part a human
PEGASUS:	winged horse
CHIMERA:	front part a combination of lion and goat, hind part a serpent, breathes fire
CENTAUR:	human from head to waist, remainder of body a horse
GRIFFIN:	body of a lion, head and wings of an eagle, back covered with feathers
UNICORN:	body of a horse, head of a deer, feet of an elephant, tail of a boar, a single black horn in the middle of its forehead

Classification Key for Mythical Animals

1	**a** Part of body is human		Go to 2
	b None of body is human		Go to 3
2	**a**		
	b		
3	**a**		
	b		
4	**a**		
	b		
5	**a**		
	b		

Going Further

Choose an organism that you would like to study. Find out how the organism is classified. Try to find out what characteristics are used to classify the organism. Make a chart of your findings. The chart should have columns headed with the terms "kingdom," "phylum," "class," "order," "family," "genus," and "species." In each column, write the characteristics of the organism that belong under the heading.

Investigating Bacterial Fermentation

Introduction

The actions of bacteria are involved in the production of many different kinds of foods familiar to you. Yogurt and cheese are both produced by the action of certain species of bacteria on milk. In this investigation you will observe how the bacteria change the milk.

Problem

What role do bacteria play in yogurt production?

Materials *(per group)*

50 mL milk	heat-resistant gloves
diluted corn syrup	forceps or slide holder
lemon juice	Bunsen burner
brewed tea	plastic gloves
vinegar	methylene blue stain
plain yogurt	dropper pipette
pH paper	staining rack
6 paper cups	staining pan or sink
10-mL graduated cylinder	coverslip
5 spoons or stirring rods	compound light microscope
microscope slide	

Pre-Lab Discussion

Read the entire investigation. Then, work with a partner to answer the following questions.

1. Why are you asked to determine the pH of the five liquids at the beginning of the experiment?

   _____

   _____

   _____

2. **CAUTION:** *Do not taste any of the substances used in this experiment.* Based on your previous experience, however, give a one- or two-word description of the taste of each of the substances.

   _____

   _____

   _____

3. Yogurt is made from fermented milk. How does yogurt differ in texture and in taste from milk?

   _____

4. What does the term *curdle* mean?

_____

5. What is the purpose of the methylene blue stain in this experiment?

_____

Safety 🔬🧤🔪🥽🔥🧪☠️🗑️♨️⚗️✋

Put on a laboratory apron. Be careful to avoid breakage when working with glassware. Put on safety goggles. Use caution when handling microscope slides, as they can break easily and cut you. Always use special caution when working with bacterial cultures. Follow your teacher's directions and all appropriate safety procedures when handling live microorganisms. Tie back loose hair and clothing when working with flames. Be careful when using matches. Do not reach over an open flame. Use extreme care when working with heated equipment or materials to avoid burns. Always use special caution when working with laboratory chemicals, as they may irritate the skin or stain skin or clothing. Never touch or taste any chemical unless instructed to do so. Observe proper laboratory procedures when using electrical equipment. Always handle the microscope with extreme care. You are responsible for its proper care and use. Wash your hands thoroughly after this investigation. Note all safety alert symbols next to the steps in the Procedure and review the meaning of each symbol by referring to Safety Symbols on page 8.

Procedure

Part A. Observing the Effect on Milk of Acidic and Nonacidic Solutions

1. Put on a laboratory apron, safety goggles, and plastic gloves. Label the paper cups Syrup, Lemon, Tea, Vinegar, Water, and Yogurt. Pour 10 mL of the appropriate liquid into each cup except the Yogurt cup.

2. Drop a large spoonful (about 15 mL) of yogurt into the Yogurt cup.

3. Dip a pH strip into the contents of each cup. See Figure 1. Compare the color of the pH strip to the pH key provided with the strips. Record the pH of each substance tested in the Data Table provided.

pH strip

Syrup Lemon Tea Vinegar Water Yogurt

Figure 1

4. Pour 10 mL of milk into each cup *except* the cup containing the yogurt. Use a spoon or stirring rod to mix the milk with the other liquid in each cup. Record your observations in the Data Table. **CAUTION:** *Be careful—glass stirring rods are easily broken.*

5. Using new pH strips, determine the pH of each of the liquid-milk mixtures. Record the pH in the Data Table.

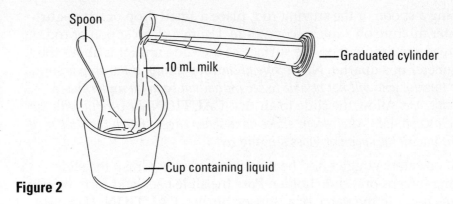

Spoon

10 mL milk

Graduated cylinder

Cup containing liquid

Figure 2

Data Table

Liquid	pH	Observations	pH After Adding Milk
Syrup			
Lemon			
Tea			
Vinegar			
Water			
Yogurt			

Part B. Confirming the Presence of Bacteria in Yogurt

1. Dilute the yogurt with about 20 mL of water.

2. Using a spoon or the stirring rod, place a small drop of the yogurt-water mixture on a microscope slide. Using a clean spoon or rod, spread the drop out on the surface of the slide until it is about the diameter of a quarter. **Note:** *Spread the drop thinly. If the drop is spread too thickly, you will not be able to see individual bacteria under the microscope.* Allow the slide to air dry. **CAUTION:** *Be careful with the microscope slide. Microscope slides have sharp edges. Touch the slide very gently with the spoon or glass stirring rod.*

3. Put on safety goggles and heat-resistant gloves. Grasp the slide using forceps or a slide holder. Pass the slide back and forth briefly three times in the flame of a Bunsen burner. **CAUTION:** *Have your teacher light your Bunsen burner. Be very careful of the open flame. Do not allow hair or clothing to come near the flame. The slide will be very hot. Allow it to cool for several minutes before you handle it.*

4. Exchange your heat-resistant gloves for plastic gloves. Using forceps or a slide holder, place the slide on a slide rack. Using a dropper pipette, flood the slide with methylene blue stain, and allow the stain to remain on the slide for 1 minute. **CAUTION:** *Many stains are poisons and carcinogens. Do not allow skin to come in contact with the stain. If it does, wash the skin well with soap and water. Methylene blue may stain clothing. Use caution not to splash any on clothing.*

5. Using the forceps or slide holder, tilt the slide so the stain drains off into a pan or sink. Keeping the slide tilted, gently rinse the slide with a very weak stream of water. Blot the slide gently with the corner of a paper towel. **Note:** *Do not let the paper towel touch the stained patch. It will remove the bacteria from the slide.* Gently place a drop of water and a coverslip over the stained patch of yogurt mixture. **CAUTION:** *Be careful with the coverslip. Coverslips may have sharp edges. Dispose of the washings from the slide as your teacher directs you to.*

6. Place the slide on the stage of the microscope. Use the low-power objective to bring some bacterial cells into focus.

7. Switch to the high-power objective lens. **CAUTION:** *When turning to the high-power objective lens, you should always watch the objective from the side of your microscope so that the objective lens does not hit or damage the slide. Raise the nosepiece to increase clearance as needed.*

8. Using the fine adjustment knob, bring the bacterial cells into sharper focus. What do you observe?

Analysis and Conclusions

1. **Analyzing Data** How did each of the substances you tested affect the milk when they were mixed together?

_____

_____

2. **Evaluating** Judging from your results, how do acidic substances affect milk?

_____

_____

3. **Drawing Conclusions** Is the pH of yogurt higher or lower than that of milk? What can you conclude about the presence of acid in yogurt and milk?

_____

_____

4. **Inferring** How might the presence of fermenting bacteria be related to pH in yogurt? Keep in mind that during fermentation, no carbon dioxide is produced.

_____

_____

_____

5. **Formulating Hypotheses** Propose a hypothesis that explains how yogurt is produced from milk.

_____

_____

Going Further

Several different foods, including yogurt, cheeses and cured olives, depend on various species of bacteria for their production. Using library and Internet resources, research bacteria-fermented foods and write a brief report identifying several, along with the species of bacteria used in the food's preparation.

Comparing the Movement of Protists

Introduction

Unicellular protists generally live in watery environments, such
as ponds, oceans, and within the bodies of larger organisms.
Some unicellular protists can move independently through
their environment, while others remain in one location. In this
investigation, you will compare the ways several different
protists move.

Problem

How do unicellular protists move through their environments?

Pre-Lab Discussion

Read the entire investigation. Then, work with a partner to answer
the following questions.

1. All bacteria and most protists are unicellular organisms. Which are
   larger?

   _____

2. Why are unicellular protists usually viewed in wet mounts?

   _____

3. Why is it helpful to begin viewing the wet mount under low
   power?

   _____

   _____

4. What structures do all protists have in common?

   _____

   _____

5. Would you expect to find more individual protists in a body of
   water that dries up from time to time, or a body of water that does
   not? Explain your reason.

   _____

   _____

Materials

dropper pipette
microscope slide
coverslip
paper towels
compound light microscope
piece of cotton

cultures of various protist species
plastic gloves

Safety 🜂🜃🜄🜅🜆

Put on a laboratory apron. Be careful to avoid breakage when working with glassware. Use caution when handling microscope slides, as they can break easily and cut you. Observe proper laboratory procedures when using electrical equipment. Follow your teacher's directions and all appropriate safety procedures when handling live microorganisms. Always handle the microscope with extreme care. You are responsible for its proper care and use. Wash your hands thoroughly after carrying out this investigation. Note all safety alert symbols next to the steps in the Procedure and review the meaning of each symbol by referring to Safety Symbols on page 8.

Procedure

🜂🜃🜄
1. Separate a few strands of cotton and place them on a microscope slide. The cotton strands will help to slow the movement of the protists. Alternately, your teacher may provide a chemical slowing agent. **NOTE:** *This step is not necessary when preparing* Amoeba *for observation.* **CAUTION:** *Be careful when handling the slide and its coverslips. Microscope slides and coverslips have sharp edges.*

2. With a dropper pipette, place a drop of protist culture on the slide.

3. To make a wet-mount slide, gently lower the coverslip over the drop of protist culture.

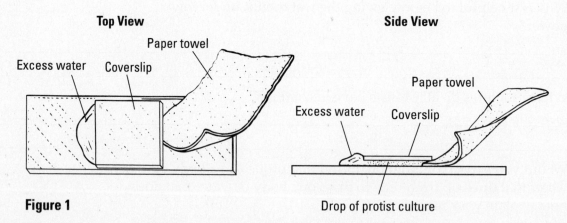

Top View

Excess water   Coverslip   Paper towel

Side View

Paper towel

Excess water   Coverslip

Drop of protist culture

Figure 1

4. To remove any excess liquid, place a piece of paper towel near the edge of the coverslip and allow the paper towel to absorb the excess liquid. See Figure 1.

🜃
5. Place the slide on the stage of the microscope. Use the low-power objective lens to bring a single organism into focus. Have your teacher check to see that you have an organism in focus.

6. Switch to the high-power objective lens. **CAUTION:** *When turning to the high-power objective lens, you should always look at the objective from the side of your microscope so that the objective lens does not hit or damage the slide.*

7. Using the fine adjustment knob, bring the organism into a sharper focus.

8. Observe the organism and draw what you see in the space labeled Specimen 1. Label any structures, such as a contractile vacuole or nucleus, that you can distinguish. In the blanks below the space, fill in the magnification you are using, the name of the protist, and a description of the protist's movement.

9. Carefully clean and dry the slide.

10. Repeat Steps 1 through 9 for a second, third, and fourth type of protist. Wash your hands well with soap and warm water before leaving the laboratory.

Specimen 1

Magnification _____

Name _____

Movement _____

_____

Specimen 2

Magnification _____

Name _____

Movement _____

_____

Specimen 3

Magnification _____

Name _____

Movement _____

_____

Specimen 4

Magnification _____

Name _____

Movement _____

_____

Analysis and Conclusions

1. **Analyzing Data** Identify the different structures that the various protists use to move through their environment.

_____

_____

2. **Inferring** Some of the protists you have observed today have been referred to as protozoans—a name that means "first animal." What aspects of these protists likely gave rise to that name?

_____

_____

3. **Formulating Hypotheses** *Stentor* is a protist that does not move through its environment, yet it has cilia. What function do the cilia likely serve in *Stentor*?

_____

_____

4. **Comparing and Contrasting** In what respect are cilia similar to flagella? In what ways do they differ?

_____

_____

_____

_____

Going Further

Based on the results of this investigation, develop a hypothesis about the relationship between protists' structures for movement and their feeding behavior. Design an experiment to test your hypothesis. With your teacher's permission, carry out your planned experiment and record your results.

Controlling the Rate of Fermentation by a Fungus

Introduction

The action of yeast is important to the manufacture of bread, beer, and wine. Baker's yeast, *Saccharomyces cerevisiae*, participates in alcoholic fermentation under anaerobic conditions. What substances and conditions promote fermentation by yeast? In this investigation, you will examine the effects of two substances on the rate at which yeast cells perform fermentation.

Problem

Under what kinds of conditions does yeast ferment sugar most quickly?

Pre-Lab Discussion

Read the entire investigation. Then, work with a partner to answer the following questions.

1. What process causes production of the bubbles in bread and in some alcoholic beverages? What gas forms these bubbles?

   _____

2. Identify the manipulated variables in this experiment.

   _____

   _____

   _____

3. What is the responding variable in this experiment?

   _____

   _____

   _____

4. In which of the five bottles do you expect to observe the evidence of fermentation? Explain your answer.

   _____

   _____

   _____

5. What result do you expect from bottle D, the bottle containing water, salt, and yeast?

   _____

   _____

   _____

Materials (per group)

5 small plastic narrow-necked bottles
glass-marking pencil
5 round balloons, stretched so that they inflate easily
sugar
salt
warm (40–45°C) water
dry, powdered yeast
250-mL beaker or small glass
10-mL graduated cylinder or measuring spoons (1 teaspoon equals 5 mL)

Safety 🖐️🥽🧤🔥

Put on safety goggles and a laboratory apron. Be careful to avoid breakage when working with glassware. Follow your teacher's directions and all appropriate safety procedures. Wash your hands thoroughly after carrying out this investigation. Note all safety alert symbols next to the steps in the Procedure and review the meaning of each symbol by referring to Safety Symbols on page 8.

Procedure

1. Put on a lab apron. Using the glass-marking pencil, mark the bottles A, B, C, D, and E.

2. Add 5 mL of sugar to bottle A. See Figure 1.

3. Add 30 mL of sugar to bottles B, C, and E.

4. Add 5 mL of salt to bottles C, D, and E.

Figure 1

5. Add 2 mL of dry, powdered yeast to bottles A, B, C, and D.

6. Fill bottle A about two-thirds full of warm water and quickly place a balloon over the opening of the bottle. See Figure 2. Make sure that the balloon fits tightly around the neck of the bottle. Mix the dry ingredients and the water by swirling the bottle gently.

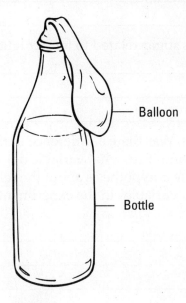

Balloon

Bottle

Figure 2

7. Repeat step 6 for bottles B, C, D, and E. Be sure to add equal volumes of water to all five bottles.

8. Place the bottles in a warm spot away from drafts. Wash your hands thoroughly after carrying out this investigation. Carefully observe the bottles each day for 2 weeks and record your observations in the Data Table.

Data Table

	Sugar	Salt	Yeast	Date and Observations
A	5 mL	none	2 mL	
B	30 mL	none	2 mL	
C	30 mL	5 mL	2 mL	
D	none	5 mL	2 mL	
E	30 mL	5 mL	none	

Analysis and Conclusions

1. Observing What happened to the balloons?

_____

_____

2. Inferring Why do you think this happened?

_____

_____

3. **Analyzing Data** In what way did the contents of the bottles with the inflated balloons differ from those whose balloons did not inflate?

_____

_____

_____

4. **Inferring** In what way is sugar related to fermentation?

_____

_____

_____

5. **Formulating Hypotheses** Was there a difference in the rate of inflation of the balloons, and if so, what variable does it appear to be related to? Formulate a hypothesis about the relationship between the manipulated variables in the experiment and the rate of fermentation.

_____

_____

_____

Going Further

Bread and alcoholic beverages are not the only food products produced by yeasts. Using library or Internet resources, research the use of fungi in the production of cheese and of soy products. Write a short report explaining what fungi are used, and how they act to produce the food.

Observing Mosses and Liverworts

Introduction

Plants without seeds are classified as either vascular or nonvascular. Vascular plants have specialized tissues that carry water and food throughout the plant. Nonvascular plants do not have these specialized tissues and therefore lack true roots, stems, and leaves. Because these plants have no way of transporting water over long distances, they must live in a moist environment. Mosses and liverworts are examples of nonvascular plants that live on land.

In this investigation, you will observe the structures of a moss and a liverwort, two types of nonvascular plants.

Problem

What are the structures of mosses and liverworts?

Pre-Lab Discussion

Read the entire investigation. Then, work with a partner to answer the following questions.

1. Which two types of plants will you be examining in this investigation? How are these plants classified—as vascular or nonvascular?

   _____

   _____

   _____

2. How do the rootlike and leaflike structures of mosses and liverworts differ from true roots and leaves?

   _____

   _____

   _____

3. How large do you expect mosses and liverworts to be? Explain your answer.

   _____

   _____

   _____

   _____

4. What is one advantage of viewing specimens with a dissecting microscope over using a compound light microscope?

   _____

   _____

5. Predict what you will find inside the moss's capsule.

_____

_____

Materials _(per group)_

moss
2 sheets of unlined paper
hand lens
scalpel
dissecting microscope
dissecting probe
liverwort
plastic gloves

Safety 🖐🧤✂️🔬🗑️📋🔥🥼

Wear your laboratory apron. Be careful to avoid breakage when
working with glassware. Be careful when handling sharp instruments.
Plant parts and their juices can irritate your eyes and skin. Use forceps
or wear plastic disposable gloves when handling plants. Always
handle the microscope with extreme care. You are responsible for its
proper care and use. Observe proper laboratory procedures when
working with electrical equipment. Wash your hands thoroughly after
carrying out this investigation. Note all safety symbols in the
Procedure and review the meaning of each symbol by referring to
Safety Symbols on page 8.

Procedure

Part A. Observing the Structures of a Moss

1. Obtain a sample of mosses from your teacher. Place it on a sheet of
unlined paper. **CAUTION:** _Wear plastic gloves when handling plants._

2. With the hand lens, examine the green leaflike structures. These are
not true leaves, but they contain chlorophyll that enables the plant
to produce its own food.

3. With the hand lens, examine the small stalks or stemlike structures
that grow up from the leaflike structures. Notice the small capsules
on the top of the stalks. The capsules contain spores. If your moss
plant does not have these structures, look at the diagrams of mosses
in Section 22-2 in your textbook.

4. With the scalpel, carefully separate one moss plant from the others.
CAUTION: _Be careful when using a scalpel. Point the scalpel away from
yourself and others at all times. Cut in a direction away from yourself
and others._

5. With the hand lens, observe the rootlike structures known as
rhizoids.

6. Now place the moss plant in the center of the lighted portion of the stage of the dissecting microscope. See Figure 1. Notice that the dissecting microscope has two eyepieces and two objectives. Because you look through the dissecting microscope with both eyes, you get a three-dimensional view of the object on the stage. The lenses of the dissecting microscope are designed to be used at a much greater distance from the stage so the field of view is several times larger than that of a compound light microscope. **CAUTION:** *Always handle the microscope with extreme care. Do not use electrical equipment near water or with wet hands. Never use direct sunlight as the light source for a microscope.*

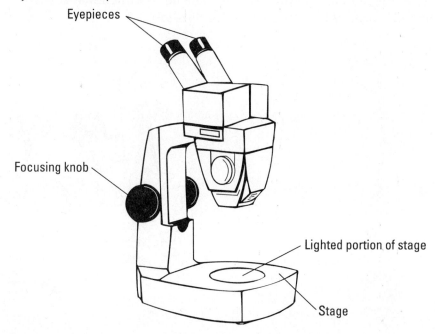

Figure 1

7. Turn the focusing knob to bring the moss plant into focus. Examine the leaflike and rootlike structures.

8. While looking at the moss under the dissecting microscope, carefully open the capsule with the dissecting probe. **CAUTION:** *Be careful when using the dissecting probe. Keep the dissecting probe away from your face and eyes and do not point it at others.*

9. In the drawing of a moss in Figure 2 on p. 154, label the rhizoids, capsule, stalk, and leaflike structures.

10. Dispose of the plants according to your teacher's directions. Wash your hands thoroughly after handling plants.

Part B. Observing the Structures of a Liverwort

1. Obtain a sample of liverworts from your teacher. Place it on a sheet of unlined paper.

2. With the hand lens, examine the leaflike structures. Notice how these structures differ from the leaflike structures in the moss.

3. With the scalpel, carefully separate one liverwort plant from the others. **CAUTION:** *Be careful when using a scalpel.*

4. With the hand lens, observe the rootlike structures.

5. Place the liverwort in the center of the lighted portion of the stage of the dissecting microscope.

6. Turn the focusing knob to bring the liverwort into focus. Examine the structures of the liverwort.

7. In the drawing of a liverwort in Figure 3, label the rhizoids and leaflike structure.

 8. Dispose of the plants according to your teacher's directions. Wash your hands thoroughly after completing this lab.

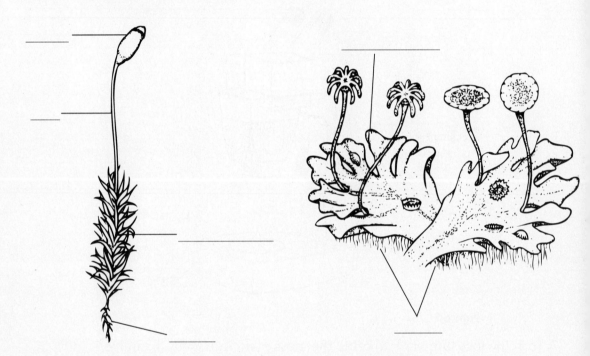

Figure 2

Figure 3

Analysis and Conclusions

1. **Comparing and Contrasting** Compare a moss and a liverwort.

_____

_____

_____

_____

2. **Comparing and Contrasting** How do true roots and rhizoids differ?

_____

_____

_____

3. Inferring Why do mosses and liverworts need a moist environment?

_____

_____

_____

4. Formulating Hypotheses Why will you never see a 2-m tall liverwort plant?

_____

_____

_____

_____

Going Further

Set up two small terraria that each contain a few mosses and liverworts. Moisten the soil. Place one terrarium in an area that receives a moderate amount of light. Place the other terrarium in an area that receives less light. Observe the mosses and liverworts in each terrarium every week for five weeks. Be sure to keep the soil moist. What effect does the amount of light have on the growth of mosses and liverworts? How can you explain the results?

Observing Roots and Root Hairs

Introduction

The roots of a plant absorb water and nutrients from the soil. These materials are transported through the roots to other parts of the plant. The cells in the outer layer of a root, the epidermis, grow slender projections called root hairs. There are many root hairs on a typical plant. The root hairs can penetrate the spaces between soil particles. The numerous root hairs increase the surface area, enabling the plant to absorb more water. Root hairs need oxygen to absorb and transport materials. If the spaces in soil are filled with water, most land plants cannot survive because they cannot get enough oxygen. In this investigation, you will examine the roots and root hairs of bean seedlings.

Problem

What are some structures of roots?

Pre-Lab Discussion

Read the entire investigation. Then, work with a partner to answer the following questions.

1. Land plants need structures that allow them to acquire, transport, and conserve water. What parts of a land plant fill these functions?

   _____

   _____

   _____

2. The roots of a plant transport materials. What are some other functions of roots?

   _____

   _____

   _____

3. Compare the functions of roots with those of leaves and stems.

   _____

   _____

   _____

4. How do root hairs help a plant absorb water and nutrients?

   _____

   _____

   _____

5. What types of plants do not need extensive root systems?

   _____

   _____

Materials

small glass jar

6 lima beans, soaked overnight

300-mL beaker

cheesecloth

rubber band

hand lens

plastic gloves

Safety

Wear your laboratory apron and plastic gloves during this investigation. Be careful not to break any glassware. Note all safety alert symbols next to the steps in the Procedure and review the meaning of each symbol by referring to Safety Symbols on page 8.

Procedure

1. Obtain a small, clean glass jar (the tall, narrow ones that are used for jelly or relish work best). If there are any labels on the jar, remove them by soaking the jar in water overnight. This should weaken the glue on the labels so that they slip off easily. **CAUTION:** *Be careful not to break glassware.*

2. Fold a paper towel into a long strip so that it is as wide as the jar is tall.

3. Use a little water to moisten the paper towel strip. Then line the inside of the jar with the paper towel strip.

4. Carefully place four to six lima beans between the paper towel and the sides of the glass jar. The beans should be midway between the top and the middle of the jar.

5. Crumple a few more paper towels and place them in the jar to help keep the paper towel lining and seeds in place.

6. Add water to the jar to about a centimeter from the bottom. Over the course of this activity, it may be necessary to add a little water to the jar to maintain this water level.

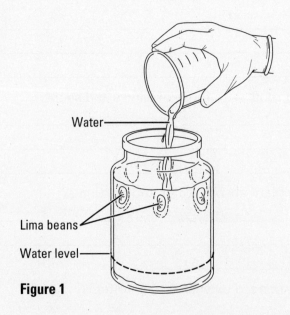

Water

Lima beans

Water level

Figure 1

7. Cover the jar with a piece of cheesecloth. Use a rubber band to attach the cheesecloth to the jar.

8. Observe your lima beans daily.

9. Examine the growing roots of your lima bean plants. Use a hand lens to look at the root hairs.

10. Draw and label one of the roots in the space provided.

Analysis and Conclusions

1. **Observing** How long did it take your beans to sprout?

_____

_____

2. **Observing** Describe the surface texture of the roots.

_____

_____

3. Observing What structures give the roots this texture?

_____

4. Inferring How does the form of these structures relate to their function?

_____

_____

_____

_____

5. Comparing and Contrasting Both roots and stems have an outer layer of cells, the epidermis. What structures do roots have that stems do not? How does this difference reflect the functions of the cells?

_____

_____

_____

_____

6. Inferring Plants such as mosses lack true roots. They have structures called rhizoids that anchor them to the ground but do not play a major role in absorption and transportation. In what habitats must plants of this type live? Explain your reason.

_____

_____

_____

Going Further

House plants can be killed by over-watering. Too much water prevents the roots from getting enough oxygen. Design an experiment to find out how much water is too much. Use the lima bean seedlings from this investigation. If the necessary resources are available and you have your teacher's permission, perform the experiment.

Investigating Germination and Seedling Development

Introduction

When conditions are suitable, a seed undergoes germination, or the developement of an embryo into a seedling. For germination to occur, water, warmth, and oxygen must be available in the proper amounts. The amounts vary from species to species.

Germination can occur only in seeds in which the embryo is alive. Not all viable seeds will germinate, even when given the proper amounts of water, warmth, and oxygen. Many seeds must go through a period of dormancy, or a period during which the embryo is alive but not growing. Dormancy prevents germination of the seed until conditions are suitable. Once all the needed conditions are met, dormancy ends and germination begins.

In this investigation, you will observe some of the processes associated with seed germination and seedling development.

Problem

What changes occur in a seed during germination and seedling development?

Pre-Lab Discussion

Read the entire investigation. Then, work with a partner to answer the following questions.

1. What information will you record in Data Table 2?

_____

2. Why is it important to use more than one seed in this investigation?

_____

_____

_____

_____

3. What measurement will be shown by the graph?

_____

4. How could you adjust the lab if you have no fluorescent light?

_____

_____

5. How will you find the average length of the root each day?

_____

_____

Materials *(per group)*

10 *Brassica rapa* seeds
petri dish
forceps
hand lens
filter paper
base of a 2-L soft-drink bottle
metric ruler
fluorescent plant light (if available)
plastic gloves

Safety ⬡🔥🧤🧪🥼✋

Put on safety goggles. Put on a laboratory apron and plastic gloves. Handle all glassware carefully. Observe proper laboratory procedures when using electrical appliances. Wash your hands thoroughly after carrying out this investigation. Note all safety alert symbols next to the steps in the Procedure and review the meaning of each symbol by referring to Safety Symbols on page 8.

Procedure

1. As shown in Figure 1, use a metric ruler and pencil to draw a line across the filter paper about 3 cm from the top edge. Label the bottom edge of the filter paper with the seed type, date, and name of one member of your group. **Note:** *Be sure to use pencil to label the filter paper because ink will smear when water is added.*

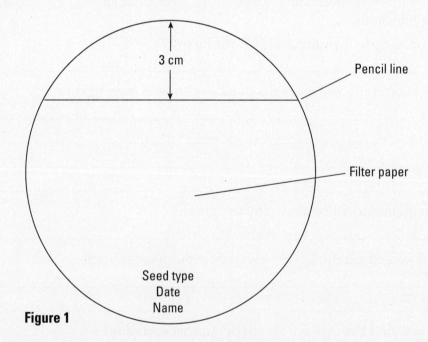

Figure 1

2. Place the filter paper in the top of a petri dish. Wet the filter paper. **CAUTION:** *Handle the petri dish with great care.*

3. Use forceps to place 10 *Brassica rapa* seeds on the line you drew on the filter paper. Space the seeds out evenly across the line. See Figure 2.

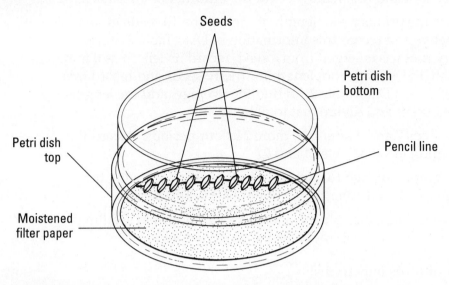

Seeds

Petri dish bottom

Petri dish top

Pencil line

Moistened filter paper

Figure 2

4. Cover the seeds with the bottom half of the petri dish.

5. Carefully place the petri dish in the base of the 2-liter soft-drink bottle so that the seeds are at the top and the petri dish is leaning to one side. See Figure 3. Make sure that none of the seeds have fallen off or moved. Slowly add water to the soft-drink bottle base from the side until the water reaches a depth of about 2 cm.

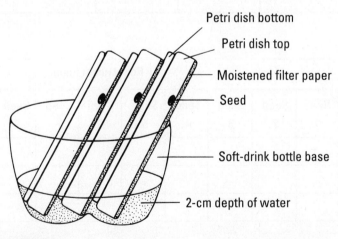

Petri dish bottom

Petri dish top

Moistened filter paper

Seed

Soft-drink bottle base

2-cm depth of water

Figure 3

6. Place the soft-drink bottle base under a fluorescent light. If a fluorescent light is not available, place the base near the best source of light in the room. Wash your hands after handling the seeds and the petri dish.

7. After 24 hours, observe the germination of the seeds. You may need to use the hand lens to see clearly. Count the number of seeds that have a split seed coat, an emerging radicle, or the appearance of a primary root and root hairs. Record the information in Data Table 1.

8. Measure the primary root length of each of the 10 seeds in millimeters and record this information in Data Table 2. If no primary root has emerged from a seed, record its length as 0 mm. Calculate the average root length for the 10 seeds and record this information in Data Table 2. To find the average, add the lengths of all the roots and divide that total by 10.

9. Repeat steps 7 and 8 after two more 24-hour periods. Record the information in Data Tables 1 and 2.

10. On the graph on page 165, construct a line graph showing the average root length over the 72-hour observation period.

11. In the space provided, sketch one of your 72-hour-old seedlings. Label the primary root, root hairs, and cotyledons.

Total number of seeds in petri dish = _____

Data Table 1

Time	Number of Seeds			
	Split Seed Coat	Radicle	Primary Root	Root Hairs
After 24 hours				
After 48 hours				
After 72 hours				

Data Table 2

Time	Root Length (mm)										Average
	Seed 1	Seed 2	Seed 3	Seed 4	Seed 5	Seed 6	Seed 7	Seed 8	Seed 9	Seed 10	
After 24 hours											
After 48 hours											
After 72 hours											

Name________________________________ Class__________________ Date ______________

Graph

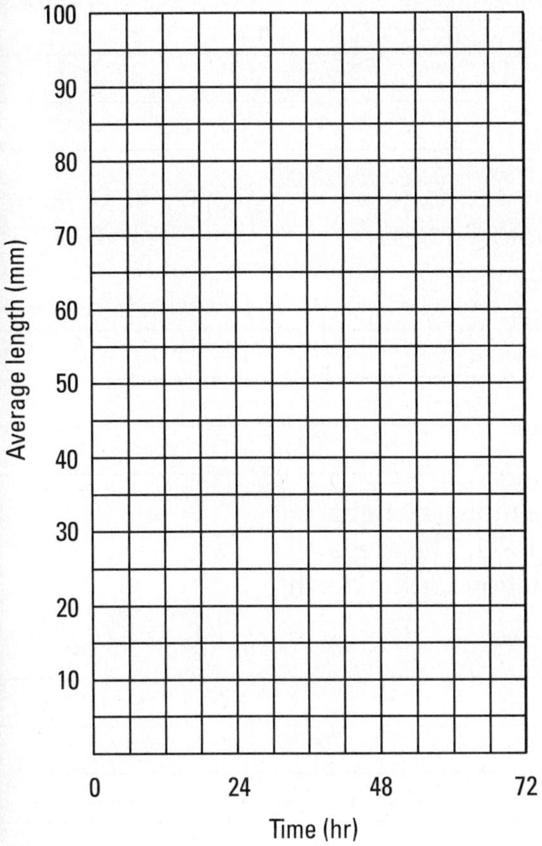

100
90
80
70
60
50
40
30
20
10
Average length (mm)
0
24
48
72
Time (hr)

***Brassica* Seedling**

Analysis and Conclusions

1. **Inferring** Why might some of the *Brassica* seeds not germinate?

____

____

____

____

2. **Observing** What is the first structure to emerge from inside the seed? What is the function of this structure?

____

____

____

____

3. **Inferring** Why is it important for the dry seed to absorb water before it begins germination?

____

____

____

____

4. Formulating Hypotheses How does the emergence of the radicle before the shoot help the seedling survive?

_____

_____

_____

_____

5. Predicting In which part of the seedling will photosynthesis eventually occur? Explain the reasons for your answer.

_____

_____

_____

_____

6. Drawing Conclusions Several seeds are put in a moist, airtight container, and the container is placed in a dark closet. The seeds begin to germinate and then die. Offer an explanation for the death of the seeds.

_____

_____

_____

_____

_____

7. Drawing Conclusions How is dormancy an adaptation for plant survival?

_____

_____

_____

_____

Going Further

To observe the effect of light on seed germination and seedling development, prepare two petri dishes using the procedure described in this investigation. Completely cover one of the petri dishes with aluminum foil and allow the other petri dish to remain uncovered. Compare the rate of germination and the lengths of the primary roots and hypocotyls of the two sets of seeds. Construct data tables and line graphs to record your observations. Explain the results of this experiment.

Observing a Plant Growth Response

Introduction

A plant's response to an environmental stimulus by growing either toward the stimulus or away from it is called a tropism. If you have ever seen a potted plant bending toward a window, then you've seen phototropism—or the response of plants to light. If you've ever watched a seed grow, you know that its roots grow down toward the Earth—a response to gravity called gravitropism. When a plant grows toward a stimulus, we call the response a positive tropism. When it grows away from a stimulus, we call the response a negative tropism. In this investigation, you will observe how seeds respond to water.

Problem

How does plant growth respond to the presence of water?

Pre-Lab Discussion

Read the entire investigation. Then, work with a partner to answer the following questions.

1. What is the stimulus you will be testing in this investigation?

   _____

   _____

2. What is the purpose of the filter-paper wick?

   _____

   _____

3. Why is it important to lay the apparatus flat over the bowl of water?

   _____

   _____

   _____

4. Write a hypothesis that this investigation will test.

   _____

   _____

   _____

5. What result would show a positive response? What result would show a negative response?

   _____

   _____

   _____

Materials *(per group)*

transparent plastic squares, 2 pieces 10 cm × 10 cm
blotting paper, 2 pieces
radish or mustard seeds, presoaked
cotton, nonabsorbent
2 rubber bands
glass-marking pencil
filter paper
bowl
plastic gloves

Safety

Put on a laboratory apron and plastic gloves. Wash your hands
thoroughly after carrying out this investigation. Note all safety
symbols in the Procedure and review the meanings of each symbol by
referring to Safety Symbols on page 8.

Procedure

1. Put on a laboratory apron. Obtain two pieces of plastic
   10 cm × 10 cm. **CAUTION:** *The edges of the plastic can cut
   or scratch you. Be careful when handling the plastic squares.*

2. Place two folded pieces of blotting paper between the plastic
   squares so that a clear channel remains in the center. Insert the filter
   paper strip in the center of the right side of the apparatus, as shown
   in Figure 1.

3. Arrange the radish or mustard seeds along the channel.

4. Plug the ends of the channel with nonabsorbant cotton so that the
   seeds will not fall out. See Figure 1.

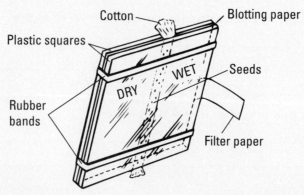

Figure 1

5. Fasten the two plastic squares together with rubber bands. With a
   glass-marking pencil, label the left side of the glass squares "dry"
   and the right side "wet."

6. Stand the wet side of the plastic squares in water until the blotter
   becomes soaked. Attach a strip of filter paper to the edge of the wet
   blotter to form a wick.

7. Rest the plastic squares over a small bowl of water with the filter
   paper immersed in the water. Be sure the other blotter remains dry.
   See Figure 2.

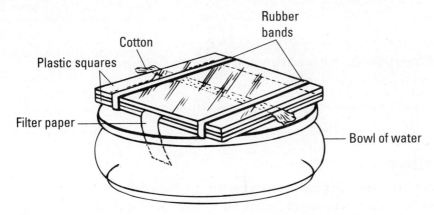

Figure 2

8. Wash your hands thoroughly after assembling the apparatus.

9. Examine the seeds each day for 7 days. Record the number
   of radicles that are growing on each side in the Data Table.

10. Dispose of your lab materials according to your teacher's directions.

Data Table

Day	Number of radicles growing on the wet side	Number of radicles growing on the dry side
1		
2		
3		
4		
5		
6		
7		

Analysis and Conclusions

1. **Observing** On which side of the apparatus did you find more
   radicles at the end of 7 days?

   _____

   _____

   _____

2. **Analyzing Data** How did the seeds respond to the stimulus?

   _____

   _____

   _____

3. **Analyzing Data** Do your data show that plant growth responds to water? If so, was the response positive or negative?

_____

_____

_____

4. **Drawing Conclusions** What advantage might the response of root growth to water provide plants?

_____

_____

Going Further

Choose another stimulus. For example, you might choose light, gravity, or touch. Then devise an experiment to test the responses of plants to your chosen stimulus. With your teacher's approval carry out your experiment and share the results with your class.

Comparing Sponges and Hydras

Introduction

Sponges and cnidarians are simple invertebrates. Sponges make up
the phylum Porifera, named for the many pores that cover the body
of a sponge. Cnidarians are members of the phylum Cnidaria. Hydras,
jellyfishes, and sea corals are types of cnidarians. In this investigation,
you will examine the characteristics of sponges and cnidarians.

Problem

What are some characteristics of a sponge and a hydra?

Pre-Lab Discussion

Read the entire investigation. Then, work with a partner to answer
the following questions.

1. Predict what the spicules of *Grantia* will look like.

   _____

   _____

   _____

2. If you observed a single tentacle, would you conclude that it had
   come from a sponge or from a hydra? Explain your reason.

   _____

   _____

   _____

3. What structures would you expect to find long after a sponge has
   died and its cells decomposed?

   _____

   _____

   _____

4. Which organism, the sponge or the hydra, likely feeds in a more
   active way? Why do you think so?

   _____

   _____

   _____

5. How does the basal disk of a hydra contribute to its similarity to a
   sponge?

   _____

   _____

   _____

Materials *(per group)*

plastic gloves
preserved whole specimen of *Grantia* sponge
hand lens
microscope
scalpel or single-edged razor blade
microscope slide
coverslip
chlorine bleach solution
toothpick
2 dropper pipettes
prepared slide of hydra, whole mount
prepared slide of hydra, longitudinal section

Safety 🔥🧤🔪🧤🔬🧤🧪🗑️♨️

Put on a laboratory apron, safety goggles, and gloves. Be careful to avoid breakage when working with glassware. Be careful when handling sharp instruments. Always use special caution when working with laboratory chemicals, as they may irritate the skin or stain skin or clothing. Never touch or taste any chemical unless instructed to do so. Use caution when handling glass slides, as they can break easily and cut you. Observe proper laboratory procedures when using electrical equipment. Always handle the microscope with extreme care. You are responsible for its proper care and use. Wash your hands thoroughly after carrying out this investigation. Note all safety alert symbols next to the steps in the Procedure and review the meanings of each symbol by referring to Safety Symbols on page 8.

Procedure

Part A. Examining the Anatomy of a Sponge

1. Put on a laboratory apron. With a hand lens, examine the external structure of the simple sea sponge *Grantia*. Find the large opening at the top through which water flows out of the sponge. Locate several pores. Water flows into the sponge through the pores. Note the long, straight spicules that encircle the large opening and project through the outer surface of the sponge. In the labeled space on page 173, sketch what you see. Label the large opening, pores, and spicules.

2. Using a scalpel or a single-edged razor blade, cut a small piece from the *Grantia* specimen. **CAUTION:** *Be very careful when handling sharp instruments. Always cut in a direction away from your hands and body.*

3. Put on safety goggles and plastic gloves. Place the piece of *Grantia* on a glass slide. With a dropper pipette, add two drops of chlorine bleach solution to a piece of sponge. **CAUTION:** *Be very careful when using chlorine bleach. It may burn your skin or clothing.* Using a toothpick, gently stir the sponge and chlorine bleach solution.

Name_____ Class _____ Date _____

4. Using another dropper pipette, add a drop of water to the slide. Then cover with a coverslip. Observe the *Grantia* spicules under the low-power objective of the microscope. **CAUTION:** *Observe proper laboratory procedures when using electrical equipment.* In the labeled space that follows, sketch several spicules. Record the magnification of the microscope.

Magnification _____

Grantia

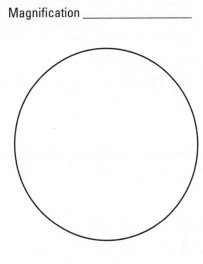

Grantia **Spicules**

5. Rinse off the slide and coverslip and return them. Wash your hands well. Dispose of the sponge as your teacher instructs.

Part B. Examining the Anatomy of a Hydra

1. Under low power of the microscope, examine a prepared, whole-mount slide of hydra. Locate the basal disk at the posterior end of the body. The basal disk is the part with which the hydra attaches itself to surfaces. At the anterior end is the mouth. Look for several long tentacles around the mouth. In the labeled space that follows, sketch the hydra under low power. Label the mouth, tentacle, body, and basal disk. Record the magnification of the microscope.

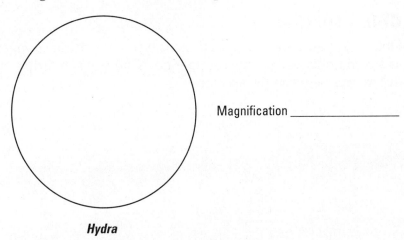

Magnification _____

Hydra

2. Locate one of the hydra's tentacles. Notice the small bumps on the tentacle. They contain stinging structures called nematocysts.

Analysis and Conclusions

1. **Comparing and Contrasting** In what ways does the structure of the sponge's body differ from the structure of the hydra's body?

   _____

   _____

   _____

   _____

2. **Inferring** How does a hydra use its body structures to get food?

   _____

   _____

3. **Formulating Hypotheses** If chlorine were added to the water in which a sponge lived, what would likely happen?

   _____

   _____

   _____

4. **Evaluating** Why should a *Grantia* sponge not be used to wash a car?

   _____

   _____

5. **Drawing Conclusions** Sponges and cnidarians probably evolved before all other types of animals alive today. What are some characteristics of animals that arose *after* sponges and cnidarians?

   _____

   _____

   _____

   _____

Going Further

Obtain and examine several different types of natural sponges, as well as a commonly used synthetic sponge. Note any similarities and differences between the sponges.

Observing the Structure of a Squid

Introduction

Squids are mollusks of the class Cephalopoda ("head-foot"). The head of a squid, which bears the arms and tentacles, is a modified foot. Like most other cephalopods, the squid has no shell, but it does contain a pen, or internal supporting structure. Unlike octopuses, squids have ten rather than eight appendages on their head region—four pairs of arms, containing two rows of suckers each, and a single pair of tentacles with suckers only at the ends.

    In this investigation, you will examine a squid. As you work, watch for characteristics typical of cephalopods and other characteristics unique to squids.

Problem

What are some structures of a squid?

Pre-Lab Discussion

Read the entire investigation. Then, work with a partner to answer the following questions.

1. What is the function of the suckers on the tentacles of a squid?

   _____

2. Squids move by using a form of jet propulsion. They draw water into their body cavities and then force the water out through a siphon. Why is it an advantage for a squid to be able to point its siphon in different directions?

   _____

3. Most cephalopods, including squids, have small internal shells or no shells at all. How do you think this fact is related to the fact that these animals are fast swimmers?

   _____

   _____

4. Snails and clams are also mollusks. How do squids differ from these other mollusks?

   _____

5. A squid can release dark-colored, foul-tasting ink when it is frightened. How does the ink help to protect the squid?

   _____

   _____

   _____

Materials *(per group)*

plastic gloves

squid

dissecting tray

dissecting pins

compound microscope

microscope slide

coverslip

water in a dropper bottle

metric ruler

dissecting probe

scissors

hand lens

forceps

unlined paper

Safety 🔬🧥🧤🥽🧪⚗️♨️🗑️

Put on a laboratory apron, safety goggles, and plastic gloves. Always handle the microscope with extreme care. You are responsible for its proper care and use. Use caution when handling microscope slides, as they can break easily and cut you. Observe proper laboratory procedures when using electrical equipment. Be careful when handling sharp instruments. Dispose of the squid specimen as instructed by your teacher. Wash your hands thoroughly when you are finished working with the materials. Note all safety alert symbols and review the meaning of each symbol by referring to Safety Symbols on page 8.

Procedure

1. Put on a lab apron, safety goggles, and plastic gloves. Count the number of arms and tentacles of your squid. Using a hand lens, examine the suckers on the arms. In the space provided below, sketch one sucker.

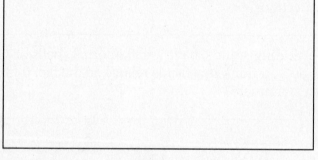

Sucker

2. Study the two longer, grasping tentacles. Examine the sleek body with its pairs of fins and eyes. Place your squid on its dorsal surface. Locate the mantle, a loose edge of tissue near the eyes. Identify the siphon, noting it can be moved in any direction. In the space provided on page 177, make a careful sketch of the specimen, labeling the mantle, lateral fin, siphon, eye, tentacles, arms, and suckers.

Name_____ Class_____ Date _____

Length of Squid _____

Width of Squid _____

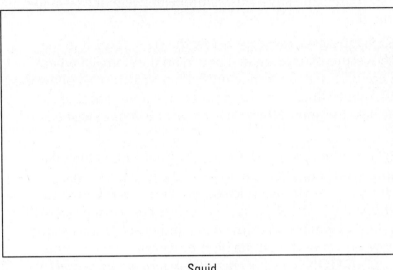

Squid

3. Measure the length and width of your specimen in centimeters. Record these measurements in the spaces above.

4. With forceps, lift the free end of the mantle just above the siphon. Use scissors to cut through the mantle in a straight line to the pointed end of the body. Spread the mantle, as shown in the illustration below, and with dissecting pins, secure it to the tray. As you examine the squid, refer to the illustration to locate the internal organs. Trace the siphon backward. Wastes, ink, and gametes are carried out of the squid by a current of water that leaves through the siphon. **CAUTION:** *Be careful when handling sharp instruments. Always cut in a direction away from your hands and body.*

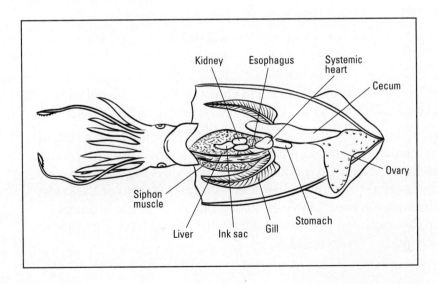

5. Examine the digestive system. Using scissors, start cutting at the neck and continue cutting through the head to a point midway between but just past the eyes. You will reach a rough, muscular organ that surrounds the jaws. Push a probe between the jaws to locate the mouth.

6. Find the esophagus, a narrow tube below the jaws. Trace it to the stomach. The cecum is an elongated pouch off the stomach where absorption occurs. See if you can identify these structures. Follow the narrow tube, or intestine, from the cecum to the anus. Identify the dark ink sac near the anus. **Note:** *Do not puncture the ink sac at this time.*

7. Examine the respiratory system. Locate the gills, which look like curved feathers, one on each side of the body. Using forceps, transfer a tiny piece of gill to a microscope slide. **CAUTION:** *Use caution when handling glass slides as they can break very easily and cut you.* Add a drop of water and a coverslip, and observe the tissue under the low-power and then the high-power objective of your microscope. **CAUTION:** *Observe proper laboratory procedures when using electrical equipment.* In the space provided, sketch what you see under high power.

Magnification _____

Gill

8. To locate the small internal shell, cut through the mantle between the eyes and look for a small, plasticlike structure called a pen.

9. Determine the sex of your specimen by observing the fourth pair of arms. In a female, there is a small horseshoe-shaped pouch or fold between these arms. In the male, the fourth pair is modified to transfer sperm to the female. Inside the pointed section of the body, locate the sticky gonad (ovary or testis), posterior to the kidneys. Observe the specimen of another lab group so you have a chance to examine squids of both sexes.

10. Before completing the dissection, carefully puncture the ink sac with a dissecting probe. Use the ink and dissecting probe to write your name on an unlined piece of paper.

11. Discard your specimen as instructed by your teacher. Wash your hands thoroughly when you are finished with the materials.

Analysis and Conclusions

1. **Observing** Describe the suckers of the squid.

_____

_____

_____

2. **Observing** List the digestive organs you could locate in your specimen.

_____

_____

_____

_____

3. **Observing** Is your squid specimen male or female? How do you know?

_____

_____

_____

4. **Observing** Describe the ink you used to write your name.

_____

_____

_____

5. **Inferring** Explain how a squid obtains oxygen.

_____

_____

_____

6. **Drawing Conclusions** Explain how a squid would capture its prey and then eat it.

_____

_____

_____

_____

7. **Inferring** Explain how a squid moves.

_____

_____

_____

_____

8. **Comparing and Contrasting** Compared with a garden snail, another mollusk, a squid has many unusual adaptations. List as many adaptations as you can, and then explain the importance or use of each adaptation you listed.

_____

_____

_____

_____

_____

_____

_____

Going Further

Examine the internal organs of a clam. See how many you can identify. Refer to the diagram of a clam in Section 27-4 of your textbook.

Examining the External Anatomy of the Grasshopper

Introduction

Grasshoppers are members of the phylum Arthropoda. Grasshoppers belong to the group of arthropods known as insects. There are more than one million species of insects. They are mainly land animals and they live in almost every environment on land. Unlike other land invertebrates, most insects have wings that help them find food and escape from predators.

Insects have an exoskeleton made of chitin. They have three pairs of jointed legs and three different body regions. These regions are the head, thorax, and abdomen. Usually, two pairs of wings are attached to the thorax. As insects, grasshoppers have one pair of antennae and one pair of large compound eyes. They have a respiratory system that provides their muscles with oxygen for rapid movement. Because they produce many offspring in a short period of time, grasshoppers increase their populations quickly.

In this investigation, you will observe the behavior and movement of a live grasshopper. You will also examine the external features of the grasshopper and identify parts of its anatomy that help it adapt to its environment.

Problem

What are some parts of a grasshopper that help it to live on land?

Pre-Lab Discussion

Read the entire investigation. Then, work with your group to answer the following questions.

1. What will you look at in Part A of this investigation?

_____

2. Name three movements you will observe in the live grasshopper.

_____

_____

3. What are the three main regions of a grasshopper's body?

_____

4. On which region of the body will you find the grasshopper's legs and wings?

_____

5. How will you know if your grasshopper is male or female?

_____

_____

_____

Materials (per group)

live grasshopper in a glass jar
plastic gloves
preserved grasshopper
paper towels
dissecting tray

dissecting probe
waterproof marker
hand lens
lettuce

Safety ⬡🖐🧤☠🗡🔥🌫🗑

For Part B of this investigation, put on safety goggles. Put on a
laboratory apron and disposable plastic gloves. Treat the preserved
animal, preservation solution, and all equipment that touches the
organism as potential hazards. Do not touch your eyes or your mouth
with your hands. Return or dispose of all materials according to the
instructions of your teacher. Wash your hands thoroughly after
carrying out this investigation. Note all safety alert symbols next to the
steps in the Procedure and review the meaning of each symbol by
referring to Safety Symbols on page 8.

Procedure

Part A. Observing the Reactions of a Live Grasshopper

1. Work in a group throughout this investigation, and write what you
observe in the spaces provided on page 183. Look at a live
grasshopper in a glass jar. **CAUTION:** *Be careful to avoid breakage
when working with glassware.* Use Figure 1 to help you locate the
head, thorax, abdomen, three pairs of legs, and two pairs of wings.
Observe the grasshopper for several minutes without disturbing it.
Notice how the grasshopper moves and note which legs it uses
when walking. Gently tap the side of the jar to make the
grasshopper jump. Observe which legs are used in jumping.

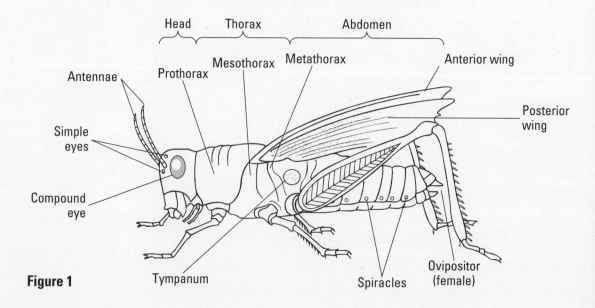

Figure 1

General Observations:

_____

_____

_____

_____

_____

Color:

_____

_____

Movement (of legs, abdomen, mouthparts):

_____

_____

_____

_____

2. Look at the position and movements of the grasshopper when it is at rest. Use the hand lens to observe the movements of the abdomen that are associated with respiration, or breathing.

3. Tear off a small piece of lettuce and offer it to the grasshopper. Notice how the animal eats. Closely observe the movement of the mouthparts.

4. In the spaces provided, write down what you noticed about the grasshopper's appearance and movements. Return the grasshopper to your teacher when you have completed your notes.

Part B. Observing the External Anatomy of the Grasshopper

1. Obtain a preserved grasshopper from your teacher. Rinse the grasshopper with water to remove some of the preservative. Place the grasshopper in a dissecting tray. Touch the exoskeleton and apply gentle pressure. In the spaces provided on page 184, write what you notice about the grasshopper's exoskeleton. **CAUTION:** *The preservative used on the grasshopper may irritate your skin. Wear your safety goggles, laboratory apron, and disposable gloves. Avoid touching your eyes or mouth while working with the preserved grasshopper.*

2. Locate the three body segments of the grasshopper: the head, the thorax, and the abdomen. Refer to Figure 1, if necessary. Use the hand lens to examine the head. Notice two long antennae—the sensory organs for touch—located at the front top of the head. Closely examine the antennae with a hand lens. Three simple eyes are located in the head: one at the base of each antenna and one in the center front of the head. The head also contains two compound eyes: one located on each side of the head. Simple and compound eyes are sensory organs for vision. Write your observations in the spaces provided on page 184.

Exoskeleton:

_____

_____

_____

Head (antennae, eyes):

_____

_____

_____

Thorax (legs, wings):

_____

_____

_____

_____

Abdomen (eardrum, spiracles, last segment):

_____

_____

_____

_____

_____

3. Locate the thorax. Notice that the thorax is divided into three segments. One pair of legs is attached to each segment. Observe the two front legs, or forelegs, and the third and largest pair of legs, the jumping legs, or hind legs. Notice that each leg is composed of the femur, tibia, and tarsus, as shown in Figure 2.

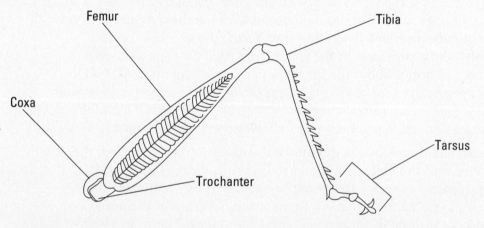

Figure 2

4. Observe the two pairs of wings. Use your fingers to gently spread open the wings. Notice the difference between the forewings and the hindwings. The leathery forewings protect the delicate hindwings, which are used for flying. Write notes about the grasshopper's thorax in the spaces provided.

5. Locate the abdomen and notice its segments. On the first segment of the abdomen, locate the drum-shaped tympanum, or eardrum. The eardrum is the sensory organ for sound. On the sides of each segment of the abdomen, locate the small openings called spiracles. The spiracles are openings in the grasshopper's respiratory system that allow it to breathe.

6. Note that the last segment of the abdomen is different in males and females. In females, the last segment is a clawlike structure with four points used to dig a hole where eggs are laid. The female's abdomen is longer than the male's. In males, the last segment is blunt and curved upward. See Figure 3. Decide if your grasshopper is male or female. Write your observations about the abdomen in the spaces provided on page 184.

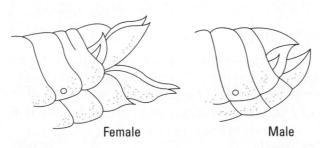

Female   Male

Figure 3

7. When you have finished your examination, dispose of the grasshopper as instructed by your teacher. **CAUTION:** *Wash your hands with soap and water after working with the preserved grasshopper.*

Analysis and Conclusions

1. **Observing** Of the three body regions of the grasshopper, which one is specialized for movement?

_____

_____

2. **Analyzing Data** What are three ways that the grasshopper can sense moving objects in its environment?

_____

_____

_____

3. **Inferring** How might the grasshopper's color help it to avoid being eaten by a predator?

_____

_____

_____

4. **Predicting** Can you drown a grasshopper by holding its head under water? Explain your answer.

_____

_____

_____

_____

5. **Drawing Conclusions** What are three structures of the grasshopper that help it live on dry land? Explain your answer.

_____

_____

_____

_____

Going Further

Obtain preserved specimens from as many of the classes of arthropods as possible. Compare the characteristics of each, such as the number of body regions, number of legs, types of mouthparts, and types of respiratory organs. Record your observations in a data table. Use your data table to identify the organs that are most important in explaining the great diversity of arthropods.

Observing Organisms in the Soil

Introduction

There is an amazing variety of invertebrate animals living on the Earth. Invertebrates are animals that have no backbones. One of the habitats in which many small invertebrates can be found is the soil. Some live in the uppermost layers of the soil, and others live deep in the soil.

In this investigation you will observe the many different kinds of invertebrates that live in the soil. To do this, you will examine a surface-soil sample and a deep-soil sample.

Problem

How many different kinds of small invertebrates can you find in the soil? What type of soil do they seem to live in most?

Pre-Lab Discussion

Read the entire investigation. Then, work with a partner to answer the following questions.

1. What is the difference between the two soil samples you will be using in this investigation?

_____

_____

_____

2. What is the purpose of the lamp?

_____

_____

_____

3. What do you think will happen to your samples overnight?

_____

_____

_____

4. Predict what types of organisms you are likely to find in the soil samples.

_____

_____

_____

5. Do you think that the location and depth of the soil will affect the kind of organisms you collect? Explain your reason.

_____

_____

_____

Materials

disposable plastic gloves
2 clear plastic jars
2 plastic funnels
coarse steel wool or wire screen
surface soil and deep soil from woods,
   a field, or bank of a pond
trowel

field guides to invertebrates (optional)
hand lens
masking tape
light source
large rubber band
cheesecloth

Safety

Put on safety goggles, a lab apron, and plastic gloves. Be careful to avoid breakage when working with glassware. Use caution when working with sharp objects. Observe proper laboratory procedures when using electrical equipment. Use extreme care when working with heated equipment or materials to avoid burns. Follow your teacher's directions and all appropriate safety procedures when handling live animals. Wash your hands thoroughly after this investigation. Note all safety symbols in the Procedure and review the meanings of each symbol by referring to Safety Symbols on page 8.

Procedure

1. Set up the jars, funnels, and steel wool or wire screen as shown in Figure 1. Label one jar A: Surface Soil and the other jar B: Deep Soil. **CAUTION:** *Wear a lab apron, safety goggles, and plastic gloves. Be careful when handling the wire screen. The pointed corner can cut you or poke your eye. Keep the screen away from your face and the faces of others.*

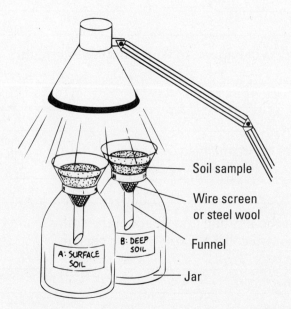

- Soil sample
- Wire screen or steel wool
- Funnel
- Jar

A: SURFACE SOIL

B: DEEP SOIL

Figure 1

2. Obtain a surface-soil sample and a deep-soil sample from your teacher. **CAUTION:** *Soil can contain stinging insects and disease-causing organisms. Keep the soil away from your face, mouth, and any cuts. Do not handle the soil with your bare hands.*

3. Use a trowel to place some of the surface soil on top of the wire mesh or steel wool of jar A. Place some of the deep soil on the wire mesh or steel wool of jar B. Cover the top of the funnel with cheesecloth. Use the rubber band to hold the cheesecloth in place.

4. Place a light source 10 cm above the jars. Turn on the light and leave it overnight. **CAUTION:** *Do not operate the light source near water or with wet hands. Tape down cords to avoid tripping.*

5. On the next day, put on heat-resistant gloves and observe the jars. You should be able to see several organisms in the jars. **CAUTION:** *The lamp will be hot and can burn you. Wear heat-resistant gloves before touching the lamp or any materials that have been under it. Do not touch any of the organisms that you collect in the jar. Leave the animals you collect in the jar during the entire investigation.*

6. Make drawings in the spaces provided of the different types of organisms found in each jar. Use a hand lens to observe the organisms more closely. Use your textbook and, if available, field guides, to identify the organisms in the jars.

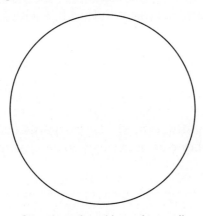

Organisms found in surface soil

Organisms found in deep soil

7. Compare the kinds and numbers of organisms found in your soil samples with those found by other groups of students. Look especially at those found in soil collected from a different area from yours. Observe any differences in the types of organisms found.

8. Dispose of the soil according to your teacher's directions. Wash your hands thoroughly before leaving the laboratory.

Analysis and Conclusions

1. **Observing** Which soil sample—surface or deep—contained more types of organisms? Why do you think this is so?

_____

_____

_____

2. **Inferring** What do you think caused the organisms to move from the soil into the jars?

_____

_____

_____

_____

3. **Observing** How many organisms did you find in each of your soil samples?

_____

_____

_____

4. **Analyzing Data** How many different kinds of organisms did you find in your soil samples? Name as many as you can using your textbook and field guides.

_____

_____

_____

5. **Inferring** Which phyla are represented among the animals in your soil samples?

_____

_____

_____

_____

_____

6. **Comparing and Contrasting** Describe the environments from which your soil samples and those of others were taken. What kinds of organisms were found in each soil sample? How many were found in each soil sample?

_____

_____

_____

7. **Formulating Hypotheses** Why might different types of soil contain different types and numbers of invertebrates?

_____

_____

_____

_____

8. **Predicting** In what other types of environments might you find invertebrate animals?

_____

_____

9. **Drawing Conclusions** What do you think acts as a food source for invertebrates in the soil?

_____

_____

_____

_____

_____

Going Further

Obtain a sample of pond water. Use a hand lens to see whether the sample contains any invertebrates.

Investigating Frog Anatomy

Introduction

Frogs are amphibians. They are adapted to live in water and on land. An adult frog's internal organs are similar to the internal organs of other vertebrates that live on land. Because it is small, a frog is easy to study. In this investigation, you will dissect an adult frog and look at structures that make the frog adapted to its environment.

Problem

What are some parts of a frog that help it live on land and in water?

Pre-Lab Discussion

Read the entire investigation. Then, work with a partner to answer the following questions.

1. What will you look at in Part A of this investigation?

_____

2. Why is it important not to make deep cuts when you cut the skin around the frog's hind limb?

_____

_____

3. After you cut and pin back the skin and muscle flaps in Part B, what two structures might you have to remove before you can clearly see the internal organs?

_____

_____

4. Which organs of the digestive system will you identify in Part C?

_____

_____

5. Suppose your frog does not contain any eggs. How will you know if your frog is male or female?

_____

Materials *(per pair)*

disposable plastic gloves   2 dissecting probes
preserved frog   forceps
paper towels   plastic food bag
dissecting tray   dissecting pins
dissecting scissors   waterproof marker

Safety 🜂🜄🜁🜃🜅🜆🜇🜈

Put on safety goggles, a laboratory apron, and disposable plastic gloves. Treat the preserved animal, preservation solution, and all equipment that touches the organism as potential hazards. Do not touch your eyes or your mouth with your hands. Be careful when handling sharp instruments. Return or dispose of all materials according to the instructions of your teacher. Wash your hands thoroughly after carrying out this investigation. Note all safety alert symbols next to the steps in the Procedure and review the meaning of each symbol by referring to Safety Symbols on page 8.

Procedure

Part A. The Head and Limbs

 1. Put on safety goggles, a laboratory apron, and disposable plastic gloves. Rinse the frog with water to wash off as much preservative as you can and then dry it with a paper towel. Place the frog in the dissecting tray. **CAUTION:** *When working with preserved organisms, do not touch your eyes or mouth with your hands.*

2. Look at the frog's head. Notice the size and location of the eyes. The round, flattened areas of skin behind the eyes are the eardrums. The two holes near the mouth are the nostrils, called the external nares. Frogs breathe in air through these external nares.

3. Open the frog's mouth and use the scissors to cut the edges of the mouth at each hinge joint, as shown in Figure 1. **CAUTION:** *Handle sharp tools carefully.* Insert the dissecting probe into one external nare and then the other. The probe will come out through openings inside the mouth called internal nares. Along the rim of the mouth, you will find a row of small maxillary teeth. Farther back, attached to the roof of the mouth, are two sharp vomerine teeth. Label these structures in the frog's mouth on Figure 2.

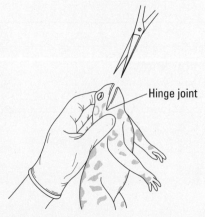

Carefully cut the edges of the mouth at each hinge joint.

Figure 1

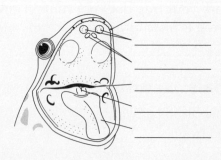

Figure 2

4. Find the wide opening in the center of the mouth. This is the top of the esophagus—the tube that leads to the frog's stomach. Below the esophagus is a slit called the glottis—the tube that leads to the lungs. Label these structures in Figure 2.

5. Use a dissecting probe to move the frog's tongue. Note where the tongue is attached to the jaw.

6. Examine the frog's front legs, called forelimbs, and back legs, called hind limbs. Look at the webbed toes. Compare the sizes of the muscles on the front and back limbs.

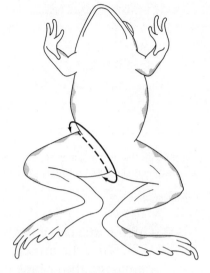

7. With the point of the scissors, carefully cut through the skin where one of the hind limbs joins the body. If necessary, use forceps to pull up the skin. Cut the skin around the hindlimb. See Figure 3. **Note:** *The frog's skin is very thin. Do not make deep cuts or you may damage the muscles under the skin.* With forceps, peel the skin off the hind limb to see the muscles underneath. Gently remove the thin connective tissue covering the muscles. The muscles are connected to the bones by tough white cords called tendons. When a muscle moves, the tendon moves and pulls the bone.

Carefully cut the skin around one hind limb. Do not make deep cuts or you may damage muscles.

8. At the end of the period, wrap the frog in a wet paper towel and put it in a plastic bag. Tie the bag closed and label it with your name and your partner's. **CAUTION:** *Wash your hands with soap and water after working with the preserved frog.*

Figure 3

Part B. The Frog's Internal Anatomy

1. Wear your safety goggles, laboratory apron, and disposable gloves. Lay the frog on its back in the pan. Use the dissecting pins to attach the limbs to the wax in the tray. With the forceps, gently lift the loose skin where the frog's hind limbs meet. Use the scissors to make a cut through the raised skin. Cut the skin as shown by the dotted lines in Figure 4 on p. 196, along the center of the body to the base of the head. Then cut the skin across from the center to each of the four limbs to create two flaps of skin. Lift the skin flaps and pin them to the wax in the tray as shown in Figure 5 on p. 196. **CAUTION:** *Handle sharp tools carefully.*

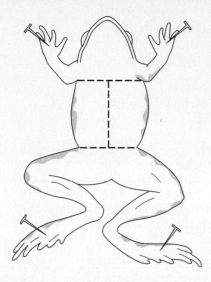

Gently lift the loose skin where the hind limbs meet. Carefully make a cut through the raised skin.

Figure 4

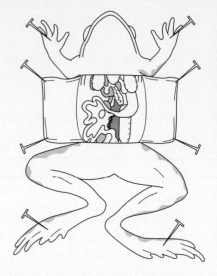

Lift the skin flaps and pin them to the wax.

Figure 5

2. Cut the muscle of the body wall in the same way that you cut the skin. Raise the muscle with your scissors as you cut to avoid damaging the organs underneath. When you reach the forelimbs, you will have to cut through the frog's breastbone.

3. Pin back the muscle flaps to show the internal organs. If the frog is a female, the organs may be covered with black and white eggs. If there are eggs, cut them away and remove them. Yellow fingerlike structures, called fat bodies, may also be covering some organs. Remove the fat bodies as well.

Part C. Digestive System

1. As you continue to examine the frog's internal organs, refer to the diagrams in Section 30-3 of the textbook to help locate and identify the organs. Find the large, lobed, reddish-brown organ in the middle of the body cavity. This organ is the liver, which stores food, aids fat digestion by producing a substance called bile, and removes wastes from the blood.

2. Use the dissecting probe to gently raise the liver. Under the liver you will find a greenish sac called the gall bladder. This organ stores the bile made by the liver before it passes into the small intestine.

3. The oval, whitish sac is the frog's stomach. The esophagus carries food from the frog's mouth to the stomach, where it is partly digested. From the stomach, food passes into the small intestine, where the rest of it is digested. Find the thin, ribbonlike pancreas lying above the curved end of the stomach. This organ produces enzymes that aid digestion in the small intestine.

4. Notice that the small intestine is looped. With the dissecting probe, lift the small intestine. Using the forceps, carefully remove some of the connecting tissue that holds the small intestine in place. The small intestine leads to a wider tube called the large intestine. Food wastes travel from the large intestine to the cloaca, a large sac that passes wastes out of the frog's body.

5. Diagram and label parts of the frog's digestive system in Figure 6.

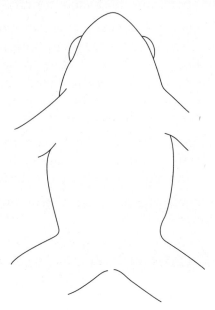

Circulatory, Digestive, and Respiratory Systems

Figure 6

Part D. Circulatory and Respiratory Systems

1. Find the reddish triangular heart in the middle of the upper body. The heart has three chambers. The two atria collect blood from the veins and pass the blood to the lower chamber, the ventricle. The ventricle pumps blood throughout the body through arteries.

2. The red, round organ near the small intestine is the spleen. It produces white blood cells and removes dead red blood cells from the blood.

3. Locate the pair of spongy-textured lungs on either side of the heart. A frog takes in air through its external nares by lowering the floor of the mouth. Then it closes its external nares and raises the floor of the mouth, forcing air through the glottis into the lungs.

4. Draw and label the heart, spleen, and lungs in Figure 6.

Part E. Excretory and Reproductive Systems

1. Gently move the small intestines to the side with a dissecting probe. The two long, dark organs embedded in the back wall are the kidneys. The yellow, fingerlike projections above each kidney are fat bodies, which store fat. The kidneys filter chemical wastes from the blood. Find the tube, called the urinary duct, that leads from each kidney to the bladder. The urinary bladder empties into the cloaca, through which the urine, eggs, and sperm are eliminated from the body.

2. If your frog is filled with eggs, it is a female ready for breeding. If your frog is a female not ready for breeding, the egg-producing ovaries appear as thin-walled, gray, folded tissues attached to the kidneys. A coiled white tube, called an oviduct, leads from each ovary and carries eggs to an ovisac where the eggs are stored until a male squeezes the eggs from the female's body.

3. If your frog doesn't have eggs or ovaries, it is a male. In a male frog, you will find the yellow, bean-shaped testes attached to the kidneys. Sperm from the testes pass through the urinary duct into the cloaca.

4. Draw and label the excretory and reproductive structures of your male or female frog in Figure 7.

5. When you have finished your dissection, dispose of the frog as instructed by your teacher. **CAUTION:** *Wash your hands with soap and water.*

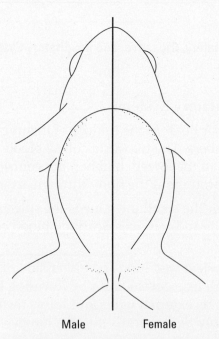

Male   Female

Reproductive and Excretory Systems

Figure 7

Analysis and Conclusions

1. **Applying Concepts** Name three things that the cloaca removes from the frog's body.

_____

_____

2. **Analyzing Data** Why can a frog still breathe when all of its body is under water except for the top of its head?

_____

_____

_____

3. **Drawing Conclusions** Explain how the frog's hind limbs help it live on land and in water.

_____

_____

_____

4. **Inferring** How could the attachment of the frog's tongue help it catch insects for food?

_____

_____

_____

Going Further

If the necessary resources are available and you have your teacher's permission, perform a dissection of another type of amphibian, such as a salamander or toad, or do library research to see whether the internal organs of frogs are similar to the internal organs of other amphibians.

Examining Bird Adaptations

Introduction

There are many different types of birds. Each type of bird has special adaptations that help it live in its environment. The various shapes and sizes of beaks are adaptations for eating different kinds of foods. A bird's legs and feet show adaptations to the bird's native environment. Birds can also have different types of feathers. These feathers, which are actually modified scales, serve many different functions.

In this investigation you will examine bird feathers and bones. You will also compare the feet and beaks of different birds. You will see how different adaptations enable birds to survive in different habitats.

Problem

In what ways are various birds adapted to different environments?

Pre-Lab Discussion

Read the entire investigation. Then, work with a partner to answer the following questions.

1. Down feathers are found underneath a bird's contour feathers. The down feathers trap air to help keep the bird warm. What would you expect down feathers to look like?

   _____

   _____

2. What characteristics would you predict for the bones of a bird that flies?

   _____

   _____

3. What is another name for the claws of a bird?

   _____

4. How many toes do most of the birds in Figure 2 have?

   _____

5. How does a bird's beak help you identify its habitat?

   _____

   _____

   _____

Materials *(per group)*

contour feather
down feather
hand lens
leg bone (femur) from a cooked chicken
scalpel or single-edged razor blade

Safety

Wear your laboratory apron during Parts A and B of this investigation. Be careful not to break any glassware. Use caution with the scalpel or razor blade to avoid cutting yourself or others. Wash your hands thoroughly after carrying out Parts A and B of this investigation. Note all safety alert symbols and review the meaning of each symbol by referring to Safety Symbols on page 8.

Procedure

Part A. Examining Feathers

1. Put on a laboratory apron and safety goggles. Examine the contour feather. Use Figure 1 to locate the different parts of the feather. The shaft of the feather has two parts: the quill and the rachis. The rachis supports the hairlike barbs that make up the vane.

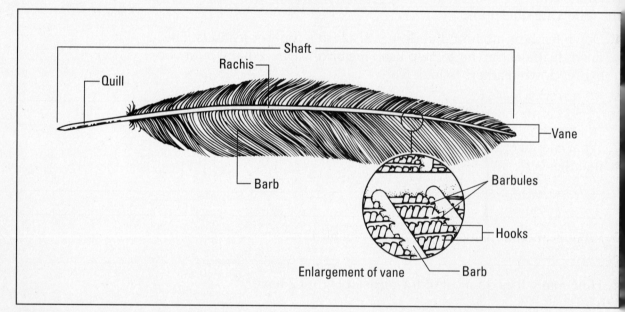

Figure 1

2. Use the hand lens to closely examine the quill. **CAUTION:** *Be careful not to break glassware.*

3. Use the hand lens to examine the feather's vane. Gently ruffle the edge of the feather, and find the barbules on the barbs. Smooth the feather with your finger. Notice how easily the barbs can be smoothed back into place.

4. Obtain a down feather. Identify the quill, rachis, and barbs of this feather. Draw what you see in the box labeled Down Feather. Label the quill, rachis, and barbs.

5. Notice the length, width, and flexibility of the shaft of the down feather. Examine the down feather with a hand lens. Try to smooth the down feather as you did the contour feather.

Down Feather

Part B. Examining a Chicken Bone

1. Observe the relative weight of a chicken leg bone (femur). Note its flexibility.

2. Using a scalpel or single-edged razor blade, carefully cut the chicken bone in half. **CAUTION:** *Be very careful when using a scalpel or razor blade. To avoid injury, cut in a direction away from your hands and body.* Observe the internal structure of the bone.

3. Follow your teacher's instructions for the proper disposal or storage of the chicken bone. Wash your hands thoroughly when you are finished.

Part C. Comparing Bird Feet and Beaks

1. Observe the drawings of the birds in Figure 2 on pp. 204–205. Count the number of toes on the foot of each bird and record this information in Data Table 1 on p. 206.

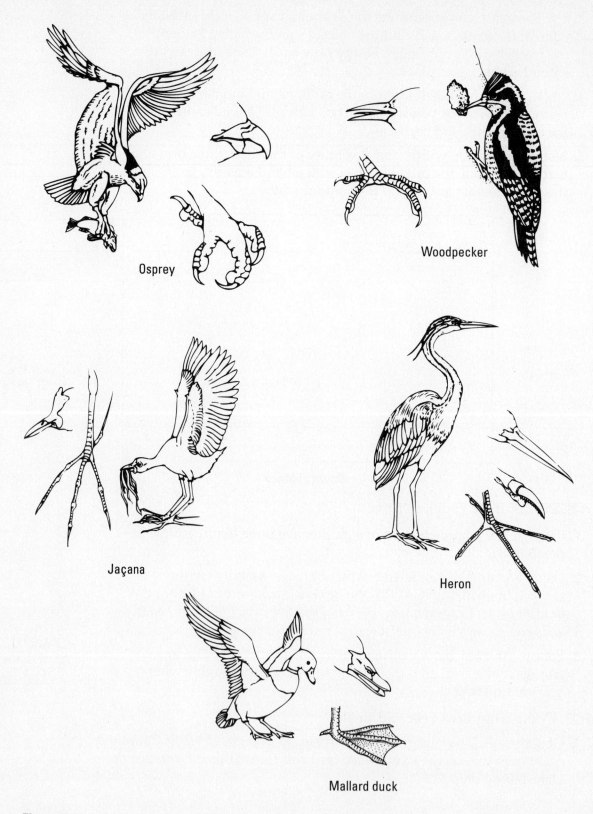

Osprey

Woodpecker

Jaçana

Heron

Mallard duck

Figure 2

Quail

Hummingbird

Rhea

Pelican

Whippoorwill

Figure 2 *continued*

Data Table 1

Bird	Number of Toes	Toe Positions	Size of Talons	Type or Function
Heron				
Osprey				
Woodpecker				
Duck				
Jaçana				
Quail				
Pelican				
Hummingbird				
Rhea				
Whippoorwill				

2. Examine the foot of each bird in Figure 2. Notice the position (front or back of foot of the toes). Record this information in Data Table 1. Describe the talons, or claws, as large, medium, small, long, thin, and so on.

3. Determine the function of each foot from the following list. Record this in Data Table 1.

   • Scratching foot: rakelike toes for finding food in soil

   • Perching foot: long back toe that can hold onto a perch tightly

   • Swimming foot: webbed, paddlelike

   • Running foot: three toes rather than four

   • Wading foot: large foot and long leg for wading in shallow water

   • Specialized foot: long talons and toes for running over leaves of large water plants

   • Climbing foot: two hind toes for support when climbing upward to prevent falling backward

   • Grasping foot: large curved claws to grab and hold such prey as fish, mice, and other small animals

4. Examine the relative shape and size of the beak of each bird in Figure 2. Use this list to describe the function of each beak. Record this information in Data Table 2.

   • Chisel: used for drilling into trees

   • Short and stout: used to eat insects, seeds, small crustaceans; multipurpose

   • Tubular: used to obtain nectar from flowers

   • Hooked: use to tear flesh

- Flat, broad, and slightly hooked: used to strain algae and small organisms from water

- Cracker: used to crack seeds; short and stout; sometimes curved upper portion

- Scoop: used to scoop fish from water; long and stout

- Spear-shaped and stout: used to spear fish

- Trap: used to trap insects in midair

Data Table 2

Bird	Structure of Beak	Function of Beak
Heron		
Osprey		
Woodpecker		
Duck		
Jaçana		
Quail		
Pelican		
Hummingbird		
Rhea		
Whippoorwill		

Analysis and Conclusions

1. **Observing** Is the quill of a contour feather solid or hollow?

_____

2. **Comparing and Contrasting** How does the down feather shaft compare to the contour feather shaft?

_____

_____

3. **Observing** Do the barbs of the down feather stick together when you smooth it? Explain.

_____

_____

4. **Inferring** How does the structure of a contour feather shaft make it well adapted for flight?

_____

_____

_____

5. Inferring How do hooks increase the strength of a contour feather?

_____

_____

_____

6. Observing Describe the features of the chicken bone.

_____

_____

_____

_____

7. Inferring How are a bird's bones well adapted for flight?

_____

_____

_____

8. Observing In what way are the feet of the woodpecker adapted to its feeding position?

_____

_____

_____

9. Inferring Write a description of the beak and feet of each of the following:

a. An aquatic bird that strains plankton from the water for food

_____

_____

_____

b. A bird that eats insects out of the cracks in trees

_____

_____

_____

Going Further

Complete a nature study of birds. Obtain a field guide to birds. Use the guide to help identify the birds in your area. A pair of binoculars will also be helpful. Observe and record the movements, feeding behavior, coloration, nest shape, and location of each type of bird you observe.

Comparing Primates

Introduction

In *The Descent of Man*, the English naturalist Charles Darwin formulated the hypothesis that human beings and other primates share an ancestor. A hypothesis is a suggested explanation for observed facts. All scientific hypotheses, including this one, are based on observations.

Darwin observed that human beings and other primates differ in many important ways. All primates have opposable thumbs. However, the human hand is capable of more exact movements than those of other primates. The human brain is larger and heavier than those of other primates. In addition, human beings are bipedal, or able to walk on two limbs. Other primates use all four limbs for locomotion. Being bipedal frees the arms and hands for other tasks, such as toolmaking. Darwin saw these human traits as adaptations, resulting from natural selection. The adaptations of other primates, he suggested, evolved differently.

Scientists have also found fossils that provide evidence that all primates came from a common ancestor. This and other observations lend support to Darwin's hypothesis of human origins.

In this investigation, you will observe and interpret some primate skeletons.

Problem

How can skeletal evidence be used to help classify primates?

Pre-Lab Discussion

Read the entire investigation. Then, work with a partner to answer the following questions.

1. How will you compare primates in this investigation?

_____

2. How will you find the area of the lower jaw for each primate?

_____

3. How many types of teeth will you count to fill in Data Table 2?

_____

_____

4. What does bipedal mean?

_____

5. How will you measure the angle of the jaw for each primate?

_____

_____

Materials *(per student)*

metric ruler
protractor

Procedure

1. Determine the relative size of the lower jaw of each primate by measuring the length in millimeters of lines *ab* and *bc* in Figure 1. Record these lengths in Data Table 1 on page 211. Record the product of these lengths in Data Table 1.

2. Determine the angle of the jaw by using a protractor to measure the angle *xy* in each primate skull in Figure 1. Record your observations in Data Table 1.

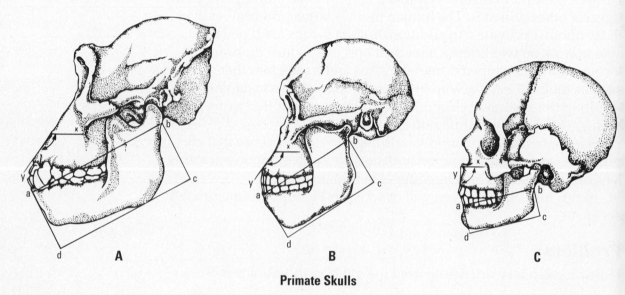

Primate Skulls

Figure 1

3. Examine the teeth of each of the three primates in Figure 2.

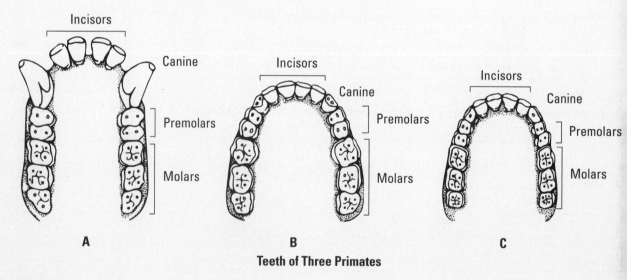

Teeth of Three Primates

Figure 2

4. Count the number of incisors, canines, premolars, and molars of each primate in Figure 2. Record your observations in the appropriate columns in Data Table 2 on page 212.

5. Examine the two skeletons in Figure 3.

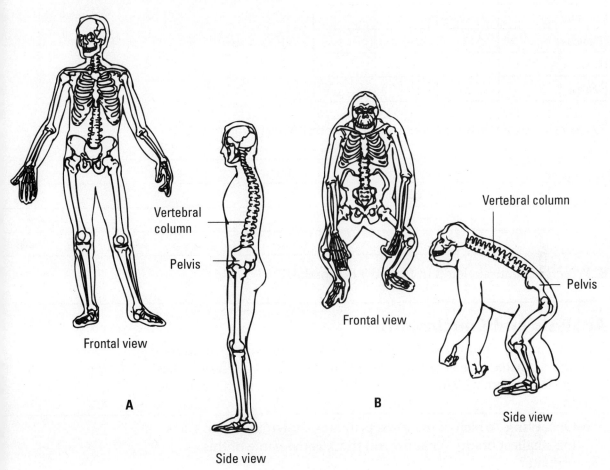

Vertebral column

Pelvis

Frontal view

A

Side view

Vertebral column

Pelvis

Frontal view

B

Side view

Two Primate Skeletons

Figure 3

6. Compare both views of skeleton A with those of skeleton B. Answer the questions in steps 7 and 8.

Data Table 1

	Comparison of Three Primate Skulls			
Skull	**Length of Lower Jaw (mm) *(ab)***	**Depth of Lower Jaw (mm) *(bc)***	**Area of Lower Jaw (mm²) *(ab × bc)***	**Angle of Jaw (degrees)**
A				
B				
C				

Data Table 2

Comparison of Primate Teeth			
Type of Teeth	Number of Teeth		
	A	B	C
Incisors			
Canines			
Premolars			
Molars			

7. Describe three differences between skeleton A and skeleton B.

_____

_____

_____

_____

8. Which primate skeleton in Figure 3 is bipedal?

_____

Analysis and Conclusions

1. a. **Observing** Figure 1 shows the skulls of a chimpanzee, a human, and a gorilla. Which of the three primates shown in Figure 1 has the largest brain? What do you think is the name of this primate?

_____

   b. **Observing** Which of the three primates shown in Figure 1 has the smallest brain? What do you think is the name of this primate?

_____

2. **Analyzing Data** What is the relationship between jaw size and brain size in these three primates?

_____

_____

3. **Comparing and Contrasting** From your observations in Data Table 2, what dental characteristics do the primates have in common?

_____

_____

4. **Inferring** Reexamine Figure 2. How would the diet of primate A differ from the diet of primate C?

_____

_____

_____

5. **Inferring** From your observations of Figure 2, which of these primates are more closely related? Is one primate intermediate between the other two?

_____

_____

_____

_____

_____

6. **Inferring** What is an advantage of being bipedal?

_____

_____

7. **Drawing Conclusions** Many primates use tools. For example, chimpanzees often use sticks to probe ant hills when searching for food. They also use leaves as sponges to collect drinking water. How is the use of tools by humans different from that of other primates?

_____

_____

_____

_____

8. **Drawing Conclusions** The brain of the human being is larger than that of other primates. How would this relate to the different methods of communication displayed by humans and other primates?

_____

_____

_____

_____

9. **Drawing Conclusions** Certain fossil evidence indicates that the primate ancestors of humans lived in areas where trees were scattered instead of clustered together. How might this type of environment have affected the development of bipedalism in humans?

_____

_____

_____

_____

10. Drawing Conclusions Describe three physical characteristics that are unique to human beings.

_____

_____

_____

_____

Going Further

Visit a local zoo to observe the behavior of gorillas, chimpanzees, baboons, and other primates. Observe the ways in which the animals communicate and interact with one another. What similarities and differences do you notice between the behaviors of the primates you observed and those of human beings? Use a notebook to record your observations.

Observing Vertebrate Skeletons

Introduction

The body plans of all vertebrates are similar in some ways. One characteristic shared by all vertebrates is the presence of a skeleton. The skeleton of a vertebrate is an endoskeleton, or internal skeleton. It is made up, in part, of living cells and thus is able to grow. It is not shed as are many exoskeletons. The endoskeleton provides support, protects the internal organs, and is a site for the attachment of muscles.

Skeletal similarities are evidence that these different animals have evolved from a common ancestor. Structures such as bones that have a common origin but different function are called homologous structures.

In this investigation, you will compare the skeletons of several different vertebrates and look for evidence of homologous structures. You will also classify unknown bone specimens.

Problem

What are the similarities and differences among vertebrate skeletons? What homologous structures can be identified on these skeletons?

Pre-Lab Discussion

Read the entire investigation. Then, work with a partner to answer the following questions.

1. What will you be comparing in this investigation?

_____

_____

2. What do the animals you will be studying in this investigation all have in common?

_____

3. What evidence will you be looking for to demonstrate that vertebrates share a common ancestor?

_____

4. Based on the investigation title and the other animals you will be studying in this investigation, from what group of animals will the mystery bones come?

_____

5. How will you determine which parts of the skeleton the mystery bones come from?

_____

_____

Materials *(per group)*

set of "mystery" bones

Procedure

1. Carefully examine the labeled human skeleton in Figure 1. The human skeleton contains more than 200 bones. Become familiar with the names and structures of the bones in Figure 1.

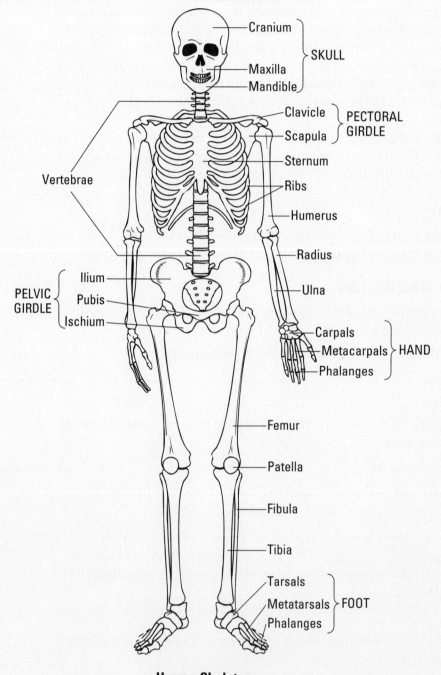

Human Skeleton

Figure 1

2. Look at the frog skeleton in Figure 2. As you examine the skeleton, compare it to the human skeleton in Figure 1. Label the bones of the frog skeleton using the names from Figure 1.

3. Repeat step 2 with the skeletons of the crocodile, pigeon, and cat in Figures 3, 4, and 5.

4. Obtain a set of "mystery" bones from your teacher. Identify the bones by comparing them to the bones of each skeleton observed in this investigation.

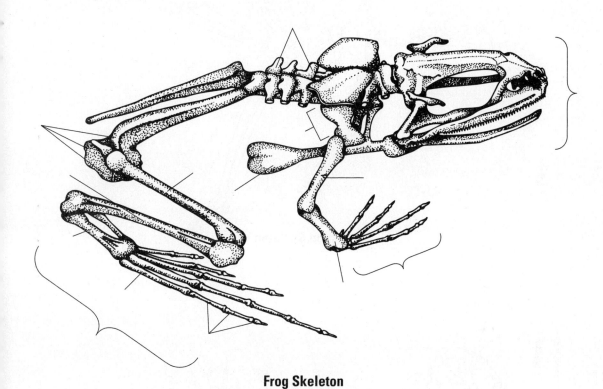

Frog Skeleton

Figure 2

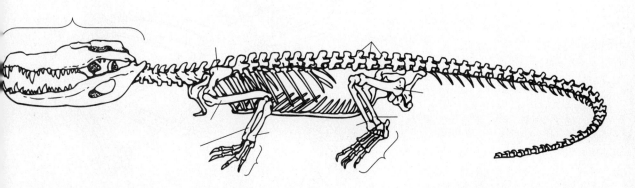

Crocodile Skeleton

Figure 3

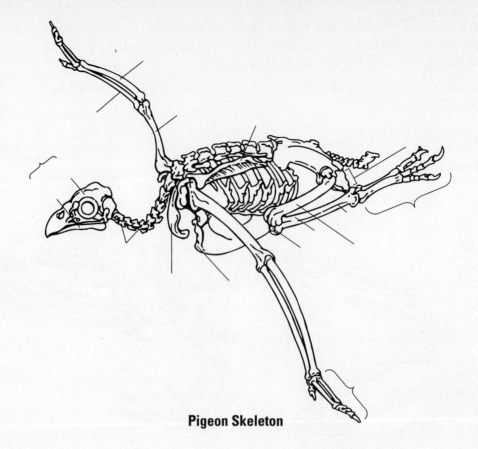

Pigeon Skeleton

Figure 4

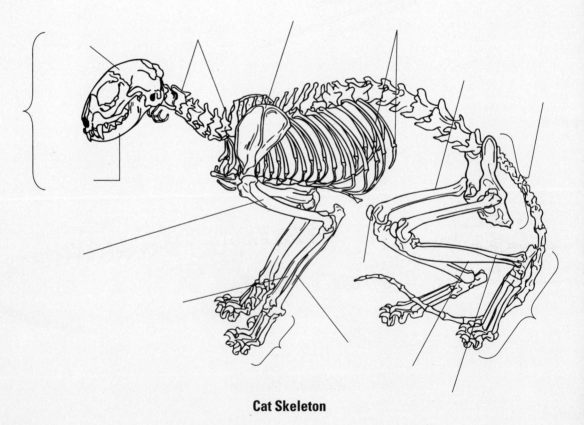

Cat Skeleton

Figure 5

Analysis and Conclusions

1. **Comparing and Contrasting** What are three characteristics that all of the skeletons share?

   _____

   _____

2. **Comparing and Contrasting** What are three differences that exist among the skeletons?

   _____

   _____

3. **Drawing Conclusions** How do the functions of the forelimbs differ among the five vertebrates you have examined?

   _____

   _____

   _____

4. **Analyzing Data** What type of evidence would indicate that the human hand, pigeon wing, and cat paw are homologous structures?

   _____

   _____

5. **Classifying** Which of the skeletons is most closely related to the human skeleton? What evidence supports your answer?

   _____

   _____

6. **Classifying** To what type of animal do you think your "mystery" bones belong? On what evidence do you base your conclusion?

   _____

   _____

   _____

7. **Drawing Conclusions** Are bones that are similar in structure always similar in function? Give an example to defend your answer.

   _____

   _____

   _____

8. **Drawing Conclusions** What evidence have you obtained in this investigation to support the theory that vertebrates evolved from a common ancestor?

   _____

   _____

9. **Comparing and Contrasting** How do the bones in the limbs of the frog differ from those in the other four skeletons?

_____

_____

10. **Observing** Describe the "mystery" bones in your collection.

_____

_____

11. **Drawing Conclusions** To what parts of the skeleton do your "mystery" bones belong?

_____

_____

Going Further

Using reference materials, find examples of other vertebrate skeletons. How are these skeletons similar to and different from those you have studied in this investigation? How are the skeletons of these other vertebrates adapted to the environments in which they live?

Observing Animal Behavior

Introduction

The way in which an organism responds in its environment is called behavior. Behaviors can be classified as either inborn or learned. Inborn behaviors are predictable, automatic responses to different kinds of stimuli. Simple inborn behaviors called reflexes coordinate internal body processes, such as the slowing or quickening of the heartbeat. Other reflexes, such as withdrawal from a painful stimulus, protect the organism. More complex inborn behaviors are involved in actions such as nest building in birds.

Learned behavior is influenced by memory and repetition. When a learned behavior pattern is repeated often, it may become almost automatic. For this reason, some learned behaviors are often confused with reflexes.

In this investigation you will observe both inborn and learned behaviors of a small mammal—a rodent.

Problem

How do inborn and learned behaviors differ?

Pre-Lab Discussion

Read the entire investigation. Then, work with a partner to answer the following questions.

1. What kinds of rodent behaviors may be largely inborn?

_____

_____

_____

2. Why is it important, for the purpose of the experiment, to avoid frightening the animal?

_____

_____

3. In Part A, if you put the rodent back in the flower pot, and it climbs out more efficiently each time, what has occurred?

_____

4. In Part B of this experiment, what is the dependent variable?

_____

5. Would you expect the rate of learning to be different for animals of the same species and gender but of different ages? Explain your answer.

_____

_____

_____

Materials *(per group)*

rodent
rodent food
thick leather gloves
animal cage
clay flower pot or glass container, 10 cm high
animal maze
clock or watch with second hand

Safety 🔬🥼👁️🧤🐾⚠️

Put on a laboratory apron, safety goggles, and thick leather gloves. Follow your teacher's directions and all appropriate safety procedures when handling live animals. Wash your hands thoroughly after carrying out this investigation. Note all safety alert symbols next to the steps in the Procedure and review the meanings of each symbol by referring to Safety Symbols on page 8.

Procedure

Part A. Observing Inborn Behaviors

1. Put on an apron, safety goggles, and thick leather gloves. Obtain a rodent from your teacher and place it in a cage. Observe the physical characteristics of your rodent and record them in the blanks provided. **CAUTION:** *Follow your teacher's directions about precautions to take when handling rodents. Wear thick leather gloves when you handle the animals. Handle the animals carefully and gently, without frightening them. Frightened animals are more likely to bite. Follow your teacher's directions about how to pick up an animal. Call your teacher immediately if an animal gets loose in the classroom.*

Type of rodent

_____

Characteristics (size, coat color, age, and sex, if known)

_____

_____

2. Observe the behavior of the rodent as it moves around the cage. For example the animal may walk, run, or stop, curl up, remain in a corner or against the wall of the cage, or sniff its surroundings. Record your observations in Data Table 1.

3. Carefully pick up your rodent and place it into the cage of another rodent of the same species. Observe the two rodents' behaviors as they interact with each other. Record your observations in Data Table 1. **CAUTION:** *If one animal attacks the other, call your teacher and ask him or her to separate the animals.*

4. Return your rodent to its cage and allow it to readjust to its surroundings for several minutes.

Data Table 1

Type of Environment	Animal Behaviors
Alone in a large area	
In an area with another member of the same species	
Alone in small, confining area	

5. Obtain an empty clay flower pot or other container with gently sloping sides such as the one shown in Figure 1. Place the flower pot on the floor of the cage. While wearing thick leather gloves, gently pick up your rodent and place it into the flower pot. Observe the rodent as it explores the flower pot and record your observations in Data Table 1. Record the time it takes the rodent to explore the flower pot, seek a way out and escape. Record the number of times it attempts to escape before succeeding.

Rodent

Flower pot

Figure 1

6. Return the rodent to its original cage and allow it to readjust to its surroundings for several minutes before beginning Part B.

Part B. Observing Learned Behaviors

1. Obtain a maze from your teacher. Place a piece of rodent food at the end of the maze. While wearing thick leather gloves carefully place the rodent at the beginning of the maze, as shown in Figure 2.
   CAUTION: *Handle the rodent gently. Immediately call your teacher if you have a problem handling the animal.*

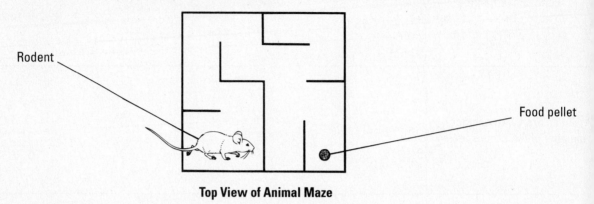

Top View of Animal Maze

Figure 2

2. In Data Table 2, record the time it takes the rodent to successfully complete the maze the first time.

3. Repeat steps 1 and 2 four more times and record the times in Data Table 2.

Data Table 2

Trial	Time Needed to Complete Maze
1	
2	
3	
4	
5	

4. Return the rodent to its original cage. Return the rodent to your teacher. Wash your hands thoroughly.

Analysis and Conclusions

1. **Observing** What did you observe in the first experimental situation—that of an animal alone in a large area?

_____

_____

_____

2. **Predicting** What factors might affect the way in which an animal behaves with a species mate in a confined situation?

_____

_____

3. **Drawing Conclusions** In Part A of this experiment, if the rodent escaped from the flower pot after more than one attempt, was learning involved? Defend your answer.

_____

_____

4. **Classifying** Was the animal's behavior in Part B, the maze, completely inborn, completely learned, or a combination of the two? Explain your answer.

_____

_____

_____

_____

5. **Formulating Hypotheses** Assume that you were to repeat Part B, the maze experiment, 100 times in a row with the same animal. Formulate a hypothesis that describes how this many repetitions would affect the results and why.

_____

_____

_____

_____

_____

Going Further

Due to the incredible variety of physical and behavioral adaptations they possess, insects have been successful in inhabiting even the harshest and remotest places on Earth. To observe the complex behaviors of ants, obtain an ant farm from a hobby shop or biological supply company. Follow the manufacturer's instructions for establishing the ant colony and providing food and water for the ants. Using a hand lens, observe the ants twice a week for one month. Use a notebook to record any social behaviors you observe among members of the ant colony. **CAUTION:** *Do not handle the insects. If the ant farm is made of breakable materials, take care to avoid breakage.*

Name_____ Class_____ Date_____

Investigating the Heart

Introduction

The heart is a fist-sized muscle located to the left of the center of the chest. The heart contains four chambers. The upper chambers are called atria. The lower chambers are called ventricles. Between each chamber, there are valves that prevent the backflow of blood. Blood is carried away from the heart by blood vessels called arteries, and carried back toward the heart by blood vessels called veins. Arteries and veins are connected by capillaries. Arteries have muscular, elastic walls to help move the blood through the body. Veins have one-way valves to prevent the backflow of blood on its return to the heart. Oxygen-poor blood from cells of the body enters the heart through the right atrium and is pumped into the right ventricle. The blood then travels into the pulmonary artery, which goes into the lungs. In the lungs, the blood gives off carbon dioxide and picks up oxygen. The oxygen-rich blood returns to the heart by way of the pulmonary vein. The blood enters the left atrium and is pumped into the left ventricle. The blood is pumped out of the heart to cells of the rest of the body through the aorta. The muscular wall of the left ventricle is thicker than the wall of the right ventricle because it has to pump the blood to the entire body.

Each time the ventricles contract, blood is forced through the arteries. This force causes a beat, or pulse, that is felt in arteries at the wrist, neck, and temple. The pulse is exactly the same as the heartbeat.

In this investigation you will examine the chambers and blood vessels of the heart. You will also trace the path of blood through the heart.

Problem

What are the chambers and blood vessels of the heart? What path does blood take through the heart?

Pre-Lab Discussion

Read the entire investigation. Then, work with a partner to answer the following questions.

1. What is the function of the heart?

_____
_____
_____
_____

2. Name the four chambers in the heart and discuss the function of each.

_____

_____

3. Discuss how veins and arteries differ in function and structure.

_____

_____

_____

_____

4. What causes the "pulse" felt at the wrist, neck and temple?

_____

_____

_____

5. What characteristics of the circulatory system increase its efficiency?

_____

_____

_____

Materials _(per group)_

cow's heart (dissected)
dissecting tray
dissecting probe
blue pencil
red pencil
plastic gloves

Safety 🧤🔪🧍🔥🗑️

Put on a lab apron and plastic gloves. Be careful when handling sharp objects. Dispose of all materials according to your teacher's directions. Wash your hands thoroughly after carrying out this investigation. Note all safety alert symbols next to the steps in the Procedure and review the meaning of each symbol by referring to Safety Symbols on page 8.

Procedure

1. Put on your lab apron and plastic gloves. Obtain the dissected cow's heart from your teacher.

2. Rinse the heart with water and place it in a dissecting tray.

3. The right and left sides of the heart are identified according to the side of the animal's body in which each is located. As a result, as you look at it, the heart's right side will be found on your left, and the heart's left side will be found on your right. In Figure 1, label the right and left sides of the heart.

4. Observe the outside of the heart. Locate the blood vessels on the surface of the heart. These blood vessels are the coronary arteries and veins.

5. Locate the two large blood vessels that enter the right atrium. These are the superior vena cava and inferior vena cava.

6. Find the blood vessels that leave the right ventricle. These are the pulmonary arteries. Use the probe to trace the four blood vessels that pass behind the heart and empty into the left atrium. These are the pulmonary veins. **CAUTION:** *Be careful when handling sharp instruments.*

7. Locate the valve between the right atrium and right ventricle. Gently squeeze part of the heart and notice how the valve closes.

8. Find the left atrium and left ventricle. Notice the large arched blood vessel that leaves the left ventricle. This is the aorta.

9. In Figure 1, label the right atrium and ventricle, left atrium and ventricle, superior and inferior vena cavas, pulmonary arteries, pulmonary veins, aorta, and valves.

10. Color Figure 1 to indicate the flow of blood through the heart, Use the red pencil to show oxygen-rich blood and the blue pencil to show oxygen-poor blood.

11. Use arrows to trace the path of blood through the heart in Figure 1 and answer the questions that follow.

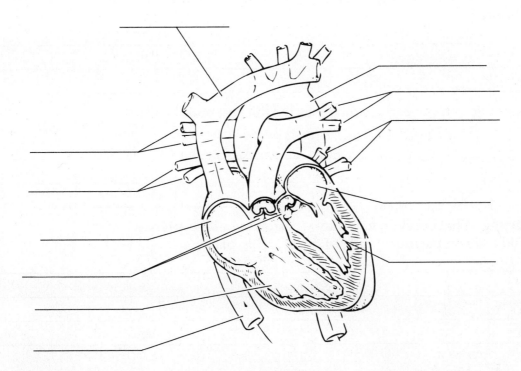

Figure 1

12. What blood vessel seems to have the largest diameter?

_____

13. How many flaps of tissue make up the valves between each of the
following:

a. Right atrium and right ventricle

_____

b. Left atrium and left ventricle

_____

Analysis and Conclusions

1. Analyzing Data Describe the positions of the coronary arteries and
explain how these blood vessels are important for the functioning of
the heart.

_____
_____
_____
_____

2. Inferring Do all arteries carry oxygen-rich blood? Explain.

_____
_____

3. Drawing Conclusions Based upon your observations, what role do
the valves serve in the heart? How do valves affect the efficiency of
the heart?

_____
_____
_____

4. Observing Which heart chamber has the thickest muscle wall?
Explain why.

_____
_____
_____

5. Inferring What effect do you think "narrowing of the arteries"
would have on the functioning of the heart? Explain.

_____
_____
_____
_____

Going Further

Using reference material, find out what an electrocardiogram is, how it
is used, and what information it provides.

Observing Mechanical and Chemical Digestion

Introduction

When an animal eats, the food must be digested, or broken down into nutrients that the animal's cells can use. In vertebrates, unlike some other animals, digestion is extracellular and takes place in a digestive tube. Within this tube, food is mechanically and chemically digested. Mechanical digestion involves mixing, grinding, or crushing large pieces of food into small pieces. Chemical digestion occurs when stomach-acid digestive enzymes break down complex molecules, such as starch, into simple molecules, such as glucose.

In this investigation, you will examine the processes of mechanical and chemical digestion. You will also observe how enzymes affect the rate of chemical digestion.

Problem

How are foods mechanically and chemically digested? What effect do digestive enzymes have on the rate of digestion?

Pre-Lab Discussion

Read the entire investigation. Then, work with a partner to answer the following questions.

1. What information will you record in Data Table 1?

_____

2. What safety procedure should you observe when cutting the egg?

_____

3. In Part B, which test tube represents the control?

_____

_____

_____

4. In Part B, why is it important that the egg pieces have approximately the same mass?

_____

_____

_____

5. Why is the piece of egg cut into smaller pieces?

_____

_____

Materials *(per group)*

egg white from half of a boiled egg
6 test tubes
5% hydrochloric acid solution
mixture of 5% hydrochloric solution
   and 1% pepsin solution
triple-beam balance
scalpel
dissecting tray
10-mL graduated cylinder
glass-marking pencil
olive oil
1% pancreatin solution

5% soap or bile salt solution
pH paper
dropper pipette
test-tube rack
plastic gloves

Safety 🦶🎽🧤✂️🧪🔥🧤

Put on a laboratory apron, plastic gloves, and safety goggles. Be careful to avoid breakage when working with glassware. Always use special caution when working with laboratory chemicals, as they may irritate the skin or cause staining of the skin or clothing. Never touch or taste any chemical unless instructed to do so. Be careful when handling sharp instruments. Wash your hands thoroughly after carrying out this investigation. Note all safety alert symbols next to the steps in the Procedure and review the meanings of each symbol by referring to Safety Symbols on page 8.

Procedure

Part A. Chemical Digestion of Fat

1. Put on a laboratory apron and safety goggles. Place three test tubes in the test-tube rack. With the glass-marking pencil, label the test tubes 1, 2, and 3.

2. Add 10 mL of water and 2 drops of olive oil to each test tube. Gently swirl each of the test tubes to mix the contents.

3. Dip a piece of pH paper into each mixture. Record the pH for each mixture in the appropriate place in Data Table 1.

4. Add 5 mL of pancreatin solution to test tube 2. Add 5 mL of pancreatin solution and 3 mL of soap or bile salt solution to test tube 3. Gently swirl each test tube to mix the contents. **CAUTION:** *Wear safety goggles when working with chemicals. Be careful not to get them in your eyes or on your skin and clothing.*

5. After 5 minutes, measure the pH of each mixture. Record this information in the appropriate places in Data Table 1.

6. After 5 more minutes, repeat step 5.

Data Table 1

Time	pH of Substances		
	Test Tube 1 (water + oil)	Test Tube 2 (water + oil + pancreatin)	Test Tube 3 (water + oil + pancreatin + soap)
Start			
After 5 minutes			
After 10 minutes			

Part B. Mechanical and Chemical Digestion of Protein

1. Place three test tubes in a test-tube rack. With a glass-marking pencil, label the test tubes 1, 2, and 3.

2. Using a scalpel, cut the egg white into three equal pieces. **CAUTION:** *Be careful when handling sharp instruments. Cut in a direction away from your hands and body.*

3. Use the triple-beam balance to find the mass of each piece of egg white. **Note:** *Make each piece approximately the same mass.*

4. Place one piece of egg white in test tube 1.

5. Use a scalpel to chop the second piece of egg white into small pieces. Place the small pieces of egg white in test tube 2.

6. Use a scalpel to chop the third piece of egg white into small pieces. Place the small pieces of egg white in test tube 3.

7. To test tube 1, add 10 mL of hydrochloric acid solution. To test tube 2, add 10 mL of hydrochloric acid solution. To test tube 3, add 10 mL of the mixture of hydrochloric acid solution and pepsin solution. See Figure 1. Gently swirl each test tube so that the liquids mix well with the egg white.

8. Set the test tubes aside and allow them to remain undisturbed for 24 hours. Wash your hands thoroughly. After 24 hours, observe each test tube. Record your observations in the appropriate places in Data Table 2 on p. 246.

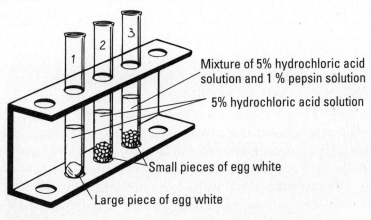

Mixture of 5% hydrochloric acid solution and 1 % pepsin solution

5% hydrochloric acid solution

Small pieces of egg white

Large piece of egg white

Figure 1

Data Table 2

Substance	Observations
Test tube 1 (large piece of egg white + hydrochloric acid)	
Test tube 2 (small pieces of egg white + hydrochloric acid + pepsin)	
Test tube 3 (small pieces of egg white + hydrochloric acid + pepsin)	

Analysis and Conclusions

1. **Observing** In Part A, which test tube showed the greatest degree of fat digestion?

_____

2. **Inferring** How were you able to determine experimentally that fat digestion had occurred?

_____

_____

3. **Analyzing Data** In Part B, which test tube did the least protein digestion occur? How do you explain this?

_____

_____

_____

_____

4. **Analyzing Data** In which test tube did the most protein digestion occur? How do you explain this?

_____

_____

_____

_____

Going Further

Label eight test tubes 1 through 8. In each tube, place 10 mL of the mixture of 1% pepsin solution and 5% hydrochloric acid solution. Immerse test tubes 1 and 2 in ice water, keep test tubes 3 and 4 at room temperature, and place test tubes 5 and 6 in a water bath at 40°C. Boil test tubes 7 and 8 for a few minutes, allow them to cool, and then place them in the water bath. Add equal amounts of finely chopped, hard-boiled egg white to each test tube. What influence does temperature have on the effectiveness of pepsin in protein digestion? Construct a data table showing your observations.

Comparing Ovaries and Testes

Introduction

Reproduction is the process by which offspring are produced. Humans reproduce sexually. Gametes are produced in specialized sex organs. In the human male, the testis (plural, testes) produces sperm cells, which are the male gametes, as well as producing the male hormone testosterone. In the human female, the two ovaries produce egg cells, which are the female gametes, as well as secreting female sex hormones. In this investigation, we will examine the process of egg and sperm production.

Problem

What structures are found in a mammalian ovary and testis? How are eggs and sperm produced?

Pre-Lab Discussion

Read the entire investigation. Then, work with a partner to answer the following questions.

1. In what way are mature sperm and egg cells different from all other types of body cells?

   _____

2. Do you expect to see follicles in several stages of development in ovarian tissue? Explain your answer.

   _____

   _____

3. If you observed the presence of a large corpus luteum in ovarian tissue, would you conclude that the animal from which tissue was taken was pregnant or not pregnant? Explain your answer.

   _____

4. For which would you use a higher-power objective—observing the structure of the testis or observing the structure of a seminiferous tubule? Why do you think so?

   _____

   _____

   _____

5. Do you expect to observe a greater number of individual sperm cells or of egg cells in the slides of the testis and ovary? Explain your reason.

   _____

   _____

   _____

Materials *(per group)*

compound light microscope
prepared slides of:
  cat ovary, transverse cross section
  rat testis, longitudinal cross section
  rat epididymis, transverse cross section

Safety

Be careful to avoid breakage when working with glassware. Use caution when handling microscope slides, as they can break easily and cut you. Observe proper laboratory procedures when using electrical equipment. Always handle the microscope with extreme care. You are responsible for its proper care and use. Note all safety alert symbols next to the steps in the Procedure and review the meaning of each symbol by referring to Safety Symbols on page 8.

Procedure

Part A. The Mammalian Ovary

1. Obtain a stained slide of a cross section of an ovary from a cat. Using the low-power objective of a microscope, focus on a part of the ovary where you can see both the outer edge and the interior of the ovary. The outermost layer of cells of the ovary consists of a single layer of epithelial cells. Immediately below this layer in the interior of the ovary, you will observe numerous round structures of various sizes. These structures are the follicles, in which the eggs develop and mature. In some of the follicles you can observe the developing egg, a large, circular cell with a darkly stained nucleus. **CAUTION:** *Handle the microscope slide carefully. Microscope slides break easily and can cut you.*

2. Examine different areas of the slide under low power. Using Figure 1 as a guide, locate follicles in different stages of development. As a follicle matures, a cavity filled with the female hormone estrogen develops. Estrogen is essential to the growth and development of the maturing egg. The mature follicle gradually moves to the surface of the ovary, where it ruptures the surface and releases the egg into the Fallopian tube.

3. After releasing an egg from the ovary, the follicle that remains undergoes a series of changes and becomes a structure called the corpus luteum. During this process, the follicle cells enlarge and secrete the hormones estrogen and progesterone, which help build up the lining of the uterus in preparation for pregnancy. Locate a corpus luteum on your slide. If pregnancy does not occur, the corpus luteum continues to grow for about 10 to 12 days. It then shrinks, eventually becoming a small, white ovarian scar. Locate an ovarian scar on your slide.

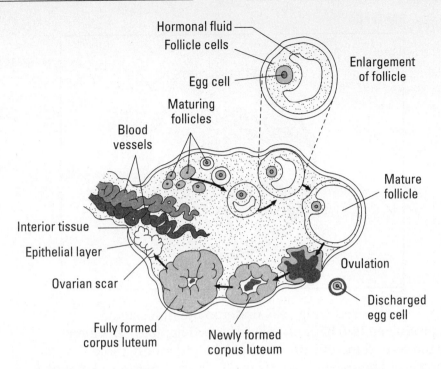

Follicle cells
Hormonal fluid
Egg cell
Enlargement
of follicle

Maturing
follicles

Blood
vessels

Mature
follicle

Interior tissue

Epithelial layer

Ovarian scar

Ovulation

Discharged
egg cell

Fully formed
corpus luteum

Newly formed
corpus luteum

Figure 1

Part B. The Mammalian Testis

1. Obtain a stained slide of the testis of a mature rat for examination under the low-power objective of a microscope. The testis has a thick outer covering and is separated into several wedge-shaped compartments by partitions called septa (singular, septum). Within each compartment examine the cluster of small circles. These are the cut surfaces of the tiny, coiled seminiferous tubules, which are involved in the production of sperm. The seminiferous tubules lead into the epididymis, a long, narrow, flattened structure attached to the surface of the testis. Sperm complete their maturation while pasing through the epididymis. The lower portion of the epididymis uncoils and widens into a long duct called the vas deferens.

2. In the space provided on page 250, label the following structures of the testis: septa, seminiferous tubules, epididymis, and vas deferens.

3. Carefully switch to the high-power objective and adjust your slide so that you are focusing on one of the seminiferous tubules. **CAUTION:** *When turning to the high-power objective, always look at the objective from the side of the microscope so that the objective does not hit or damage the slide.*

4. Notice that the walls of the seminiferous tubule consist of many layers of cells. The cytoplasm of these cells will most likely be stained red and the chromosomes in the nuclei will most likely be stained blue. Closely examine these cells in order to trace the various stages of sperm cell production. The cells nearest to the outer surface of the seminiferous tubule are the sperm-producing cells. These cells divide by mitosis. Half of the daughter cells remain sperm-producing cells, while the other half undergo meiosis and become sperm. These cells make up the layer next to the sperm-producing cells.

Rat Testis

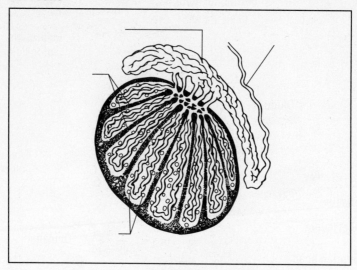

5. The diploid sperm-producing cells undergo the first stage of meiosis, producing two haploid cells. The two haploid cells then undergo the second meiotic division, producing four haploid spermatid cells. The spermatid cells make up the innermost layer of the seminiferous tubule. A spermatid cell develops into a sperm with an oval head and a long, whiplike tail.

6. Observe how the sperm cells are clustered around elongated cells that are evenly spaced around the circumference of the seminiferous tubule. These elongated cells probably provide nutrients for the developing sperm cells. Observe how the tails of the sperm cells point into the central opening of the seminiferous tubule.

7. In the space provided, label the following parts of the seminiferous tubule: sperm-producing cells, spermatids, sperm cells, and elongated cells.

Rat Seminiferous Tubule

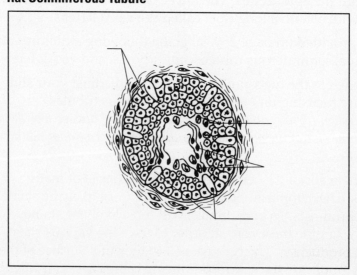

8. Obtain a prepared slide of a cross section of the epididymis of a mature rat. Observe the epididymis under low and then high power. Note the sperm cells clustered within the central opening of the epididymis. Observe that the cells lining the central opening are lined with cilia. These cilia help propel the sperm cells through the epididymis. Observe the smooth muscle cells in the walls of the epididymis. As these muscles contract, the sperm cells are pushed through the epididymis, toward the vas deferens.

9. In the space provided, label the following parts of the epididymis: central opening, sperm cells, cilia, and smooth muscle cells.

Rat Epididymis

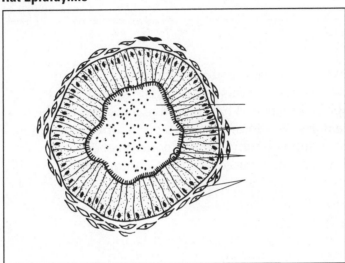

Analysis and Conclusions

1. **Observing** In the ovarian tissue, how many follicles in various stages of development did you observe?

_____

_____

_____

2. **Inferring** Considering that cats give birth to litters rather than single kittens, in what way does ovulation in cats differ from ovulation in humans?

_____

_____

_____

3. **Evaluating** Is it reasonable to refer to the corpus luteum as an endocrine structure? Explain your answer.

_____

_____

_____

4. **Comparing and Contrasting** Compare an egg cell to a sperm cell. In what ways are they similar? In what ways do they differ?

_____

_____

_____

5. **Formulating Hypotheses** The middle section of a sperm cell is packed with mitochondria. Use your knowledge of mitochondria to hypothesize the primary purpose that they serve in the sperm cell.

_____

_____

_____

Going Further

Infertility is a problem faced by some couples who desire to have children. Identify possible causes of this problem. Is it simply the inability to produce sperm or eggs? What corrective measures can be taken for males and females? Do library research on in vitro fertilization. Be sure to include information on why the technique is used, what procedures are involved, and how successful the technique is.

Name_____ Class_____ Date _____

Constructing Models of Antibodies

Introduction

The immune system is able to protect the body from pathogens such as bacteria and viruses. This response depends on special proteins called antibodies. Antibodies are Y-shaped proteins, composed of four polypeptides, two light and two heavy chains. These polypeptides are held together by disulfide bonds (S-S). Production of antibodies occurs in response to the presence of antigens. An antigen is any substance on the surface of a pathogen that provokes a response from the immune system. Each pathogen possesses specific antigens on its surface. In turn, the antibodies are also specific, binding to particular antigens and forming a clump that is destroyed by white blood cells. In this investigation, you will construct a model of an antibody molecule in order to better understand their structure and function.

Problem

What is the structure of antibodies and how does it relate to their function?

Pre-Lab Discussion

Read the entire investigation. Then, work with a partner to answer the following questions.

1. What are antigens and where are they found?

_____

_____

2. What are antibodies and when are they produced?

_____

_____

3. What is the basic structure of an antibody?

_____

_____

4. How does an antibody help to get rid of a pathogen?

_____

_____

5. What special feature must an antibody have in order to bind to specific pathogens?

_____

_____

Materials *(per group)*

3 different-colored pieces of construction paper (red, yellow, and a third color)
metric ruler
pencil
scissors
transparent tape
paper clips (4)

Safety ✂

Be careful when handling sharp instruments. Note the safety alert
symbol next to step 2 in the Procedure and review the meaning of the
symbol by referring to Safety Symbols on page 8.

Procedure

1. Use Figure 1 as a guide.

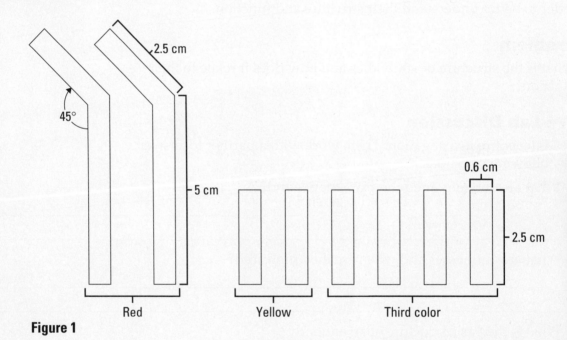

Figure 1

✂ 2. On the red piece of construction paper, draw the images labeled
   "Red" in Figure 1. Use the metric ruler to make the measurements.
   There should be approximately a 45-degree bend one third of the
   way down the strip as shown in Figure 1. Cut out the two images.

3. Cut two strips of yellow construction paper measuring 2.5 cm × 0.6
   cm each.

4. Your teacher will provide each group with a third color of
   construction paper. Cut four strips of the third color paper
   measuring 2.5 cm × 0.6 cm.

5. Line up the strips of paper and follow the steps below to construct the model as shown in Figure 2.

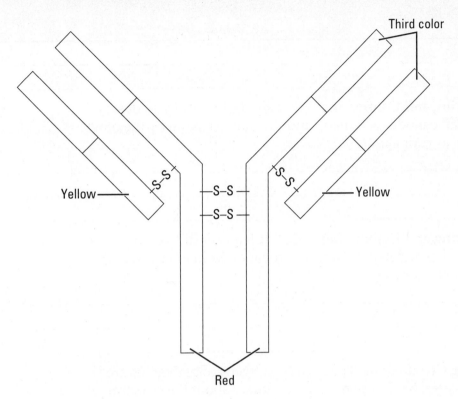

Figure 2

6. To produce one light chain, tape a yellow strip to a third color strip. Repeat to form the second light chain.

7. To produce one heavy chain, tape a strip of the third color to the end of a red strip that it is closer to the bend. Repeat to produce the other heavy chain.

8. Referring again to Figure 2, produce one half of the antibody molecule by orienting one of the long chains like a half-Y. Line up one of the light chains next to the outside of the heavy chain so that the ends of the third color are adjacent.

9. Use paper clips to represent disulfide bonds, (represented in Figure 2 as –S-S–). Connect the light and heavy chains with a paper clip just above the bend.

10. Repeat steps 7 and 8 to produce the other half-Y of the antibody molecule.

11. Complete the antibody molecule by connecting the two half-Y's of the molecule to form a Y shape. Connect the two halves just below the bend in the Y using the two remaining paper clips to represent two disulfide bonds as shown in Figure 2.

12. Compare your model to the models constructed by the other students in the class.

Analysis and Conclusions

1. **Analyzing Data** Describe the overall shape and structure of antibodies.

_____

_____

_____

2. **Comparing and Contrasting** What similarities did you observe between the model you made and the models made by the other students in your class?

_____

_____

_____

3. **Comparing and Contrasting** What differences did you observe between the model you made and the models made by the other students in your class?

_____

_____

_____

4. **Drawing Conclusions** The surface antigens of pathogens are quite diverse. Based upon what you know about the structure of antibodies, which part of an antibody molecule binds to an antigen? Explain your answer.

_____

_____

_____

_____

Going Further

There are 22 different amino acids in proteins. Calculate the number of possible amino acid sequences in a variable region of an antibody molecule 6 amino acids long. Evaluate whether this would be enough diversity for the many antigens a person might encounter in his or her lifetime.